# University of Michigan Business School Management Series

**INNOVATIVE SOLUTIONS TO THE PRESSING PROBLEMS OF BUSINESS**

The mission of the University of Michigan Business School Management Series is to provide accessible, practical, and cutting-edge solutions to the most critical challenges facing business-people today. The UMBS Management Series provides concepts and tools for people who seek to make a significant difference in their organizations. Drawing on the research and experience of faculty at the University of Michigan Business School, the books are written to stretch thinking while providing practical, focused, and innovative solutions to the pressing problems of business.

**Also available in the UMBS series:**

*Becoming a Better Value Creator,* by Anjan V. Thakor

*Achieving Success Through Social Capital,* by Wayne Baker

*Improving Customer Satisfaction, Loyalty, and Profit,*
by Michael D. Johnson and Anders Gustafsson

*The Compensation Solution,* by John E. Tropman

*Strategic Interviewing,* by Richaurd Camp, Mary Vielhaber,
and Jack L. Simonetti

*Creating the Multicultural Organization,* by Taylor Cox

*Getting Results,* by Clinton O. Longenecker and
Jack L. Simonetti

*A Company of Leaders,* by Gretchen M. Spreitzer and
Robert E. Quinn

*Managing the Unexpected,* by Karl Weick and Kathleen Sutcliffe

*Using the Law for Competitive Advantage,* by George J. Siedel

*Creativity at Work,* by Jeff DeGraff and Katherine A. Lawrence

*Making I/T Work,* by Dennis G. Severance and Jacque Passino

*Decision Management,* by J. Frank Yates

*A Manager's Guide to Employment Law,* by Dana M. Muir

*The Ethical Challenge,* edited by Noel M. Tichy and
Andrew R. McGill

For additional information on any of these titles or future
titles in the series, visit www.umbsbooks.com.

# Executive Summary

This book shows how to create a competitive advantage through service development and innovation. For executives who set service strategy and managers in charge of implementing the process, it provides the frameworks and tools to compete successfully in a service economy. Its approach is useful to traditional service companies as well as those manufacturing companies that are moving down the value chain to include services as part of their customer offering.

Chapter One describes the importance and evolution of service in our economies and what makes services different from products. Case studies involving SAS, an international airline, and Sterling Pulp Chemicals, a supplier to the chemical industry, show the important role that services play in creating a sustainable competitive advantage.

Chapter Two describes a strategy for developing a service advantage:

- *Build the culture.* Believe as an organization that certain ways of doing business are essential to long-run performance.
- *Stay focused.* Decide whom to serve and whom not to serve.
- *Link activities.* Create a seamless system of linked activities that solves customer problems or provides unique experiences.

The story of IKEA, a global furniture retailer, illustrates how a company built on a strong culture that stays focused on its market segment can link activities over time to become a formidable competitor.

The next three chapters relate the strategy to three different stages of what we call the hierarchy of service development. For each stage, they provide step-by-step processes and tools. Chapter Three presents an approach to service maintenance as a process of removing things gone wrong. The nature of service production means that things will go wrong during service delivery that require attention. A number of tools can be used to identify service defects that need correction and that provide input for an ongoing service improvement cycle.

Moving beyond the correction of defects, Chapter Four describes a process for improving service performance. This includes understanding the drivers of satisfaction and loyalty, setting priorities for improvement and innovation, and linking new activities through service development.

As fellow engineers in the service process, customers are unencumbered by your organization and its constraints. Chapter Five describes how to take advantage of the essential role that customers play in generating service ideas and developing innovative service designs.

Chapter Six provides important insights regarding your role as a leader in the overall service development process.

# Competing in a Service Economy

How to Create a
Competitive Advantage
Through Service
Development and
Innovation

Anders Gustafsson
Michael D. Johnson

JOSSEY-BASS
A Wiley Imprint
www.josseybass.com

Published by Jossey-Bass
A Wiley Imprint
989 Market Street, San Francisco, CA 94103-1741   www.josseybass.com

Jossey-Bass books and products are available through most bookstores. To contact Jossey-Bass directly call our Customer Care Department within the U.S. at 800-956-7739, outside the U.S. at 317-572-3986 or fax 317-572-4002.

Jossey-Bass also publishes its books in a variety of electronic formats. Some content that appears in print may not be available in electronic books.

*Credits:*

Page from IKEA.com, on p. 114, is reproduced with permission of Inter IKEA Systems B.V.

Gate Café concept illustrations, on p. 138, are copyright Doblin Inc.

"The IKEA Saga: How Service Culture Drives Strategy" is reprinted in the appendix with permission of the authors and the publisher, Frank Cass Publishers, London.

**Library of Congress Cataloging-in-Publication Data**
Gustafsson, Anders
    Competing in a service economy: how to create a competitive advantage through service development and innovation / Anders Gustafsson, Michael D. Johnson.—1st ed.
        p. cm.—(The University of Michigan Business School management series)
    Includes bibliographical references.
        ISBN 0-7879-6156-6 (alk. paper)
    1. Customer services—Management. 2. Service industries—Technological innovations—Management. 3. Competition. I. Johnson, Michael D., date. II. Title. III. Series.
    HF5415.5J637 2003
    658.8'12—dc21

                                                            2002155591

Printed in the United States of America
FIRST EDITION
*HB Printing*   10 9 8 7 6 5 4 3 2 1

# Contents

To our colleagues at CTF:
The Centrum för Tjänsteforskning
(Service Research Center)
at Karlstad University, Sweden

# Series Foreword

Welcome to the University of Michigan Business School Management Series. The books in this series address the most urgent problems facing business today. The series is part of a larger initiative at the University of Michigan Business School (UMBS) that ties together a range of efforts to create and share knowledge through conferences, survey research, interactive and distance training, print publications, and news media.

It is just this type of broad-based initiative that sparked my love affair with UMBS in 1984. From the day I arrived I was enamored with the quality of the research, the quality of the MBA program, and the quality of the Executive Education Center. Here was a business school committed to new lines of research, new ways of teaching, and the practical application of ideas. It was a place where innovative thinking could result in tangible outcomes.

The UMBS Management Series is one very important outcome, and it has an interesting history. It turns out that every year five thousand participants in our executive program fill out a marketing survey in which they write statements indicating the most important problems they face. One day Lucy Chin, one of our administrators, handed me a document containing all these statements. A content analysis of the data resulted in a list of forty-five pressing problems. The topics ranged from growing a company to managing personal stress. The list covered a wide territory, and I started to see its potential. People in organizations tend to be driven by a very traditional set of problems, but the solutions evolve. I went to my friends at Jossey-Bass to discuss a publishing project. The discussion eventually grew into the University of Michigan Business School Management Series— Innovative Solutions to the Pressing Problems of Business.

The books are independent of each other, but collectively they create a comprehensive set of management tools that cut across all the functional areas of business—from strategy to human resources to finance, accounting, and operations. They draw on the interdisciplinary research of the Michigan faculty. Yet each book is written so a serious manager can read it quickly and act immediately. I think you will find that they are books that will make a significant difference to you and your organization.

*Robert E. Quinn, Consulting Editor*
*M.E. Tracy Distinguished Professor*
*University of Michigan Business School*

# Preface

Services have come to dominate our economies. Whether you manage a traditional service firm or a manufacturing company, adding value through services has become an essential way to compete. This evolution toward services is a function of increased time demands, the availability of self-service technologies, the growth of outsourcing and networking, and increased competition. The evolution of competition forces you to compete on more than just product value. Today customers are looking for service value, comprehensive solutions, and memorable experiences.

Our experience with a variety of both manufacturing and service organizations reveals a stark contrast. Whereas physical goods emerge from a structured development process, new service ideas are lucky to emerge from what is, at best, an ad hoc process. Increasing your success rate for new services requires more than just taking systems that work in a product context and applying them to services. Don't kid yourself—services are very different. Our motivation in writing this book is to bring structure to the process of new service development and innovation in a way that recognizes just what makes services and service customers unique.

In our first contribution to the University of Michigan Business School Management Series (*Improving Customer Satisfaction, Loyalty, and Profit: An Integrated Measurement and Management System*), we described how to develop a customer satisfaction measurement and management system. This second contribution to the series builds on our earlier work by focusing on how all of a company's improvement systems work together in a service context.

The book is intended for executives and managers with direct responsibility for developing a service strategy and putting systems in place to make it work. If you are an executive, your job is to set strategy and enable employees to continuously improve. If you are a front-line manager, your job is to better understand the problems your customers are trying to solve and how your company can help them. Our approach helps you meet these challenges through a strategy of service improvement and innovation that creates and sustains a competitive service advantage. Excellent service firms pursue a three-part strategy: build the culture, stay focused, and link activities. This strategy provides the basis for a number of tools that support an ongoing process of service maintenance, improving service performance, and service innovation.

Throughout, the book emphasizes the role that customers play as coworkers and fellow engineers in the service process. As you will see, they are indeed an essential source of information, innovation, and creativity. Cases and other research into the practices of such companies as IKEA, Ritz-Carlton, Sterling Pulp Chemicals, and SAS will show how successful service providers have immersed themselves in customers to link activities consistent with the company's culture and market focus.

The book's discussion of service strategies and practices will also yield some important lessons regarding your role as a leader in the process. These insights will center around the importance of living your company's culture, managing by walking around, emphasizing creativity, and remaining focused on your market segment.

## ■ Acknowledgments

Many people have been critical to our success. We dedicate the book to our colleagues at CTF (Centrum för Tjänsteforskning, or Service Research Center) at Karlstad University in Sweden. Without the CTF research team this book would simply not have been possible. We especially thank Bo Edvardsson for both his support and his contribution to our ideas. We thank Bob Quinn of the University of Michigan Business School for his commitment to making the school's Management Series such a great success. We thank the Jossey-Bass team, including Cedric Crocker, Byron Schneider, and especially our editor Kathe Sweeney, for making this project a reality. This book has benefited tremendously from the inclusion of cases and examples from various companies and organizations, including Disney, Ericsson, IKEA, the National Association of Convenience Stores, Ritz-Carlton, Scandinavian Airline Systems, Sterling Pulp Chemicals, and Telia Mobile. Very special thanks go out to Alan Venable. This is the second time we have worked closely with Alan as a developmental editor through multiple drafts. His talent and attention to detail continue to teach us a better way to communicate.

Finally, to our spouses, Lena and Jill Marie, and our children, Amie, Samuel, Alexander, Andrew, and Thomas, we thank you for the love and support that keeps us going. These past six years of working together and watching our families grow have been a highlight of our lives.

*March 2003*

Anders Gustafsson
*Karlstad, Sweden*

Michael D. Johnson
*Ann Arbor, Michigan*

# Competing in a Service Economy

# Competing Through Services

Competing through services has become more than just a trend. Whether you compete in a traditional service industry or produce physical goods, adding value through services has become a way of life. As an executive, your job is to set a service strategy and enable your people to both innovate and continuously improve your services. As a front-line service manager or even an engineer in the field, your job is to better understand your customers and the problems they are trying to solve, and to improve their lives. Whether your role is that of enabler or doer, the delivery of high-quality services is your responsibility. The business logic of competing through services is simple: solving customer problems with cost-effective service solutions is the best way to keep your customers from doing business with somebody else.

What is driving managers' attention to focus on service competition? And what makes services and service management different from products and product management? Here in Chapter One we address these questions and the role that service competition plays in the evolution of management thought. Through two case studies we illustrate the important roles that services and service development play for both a traditional service company (an airline) and a physical goods producer (a chemical company). The end of the chapter introduces our general approach to developing a competitive service advantage and describes a framework for service development. The framework serves as a blueprint for the rest of the book.

## ■ The Importance of Services

Why is service so important to your company's success? The most obvious reason is that services have come to dominate our economies. In the United States alone, the percentage of service output as a share of gross domestic product has grown from 38 percent in 1959 to over 55 percent today; services as a share of personal consumption expenditures have grown from 40 percent to over 60 percent for the same period.[1] From hotels and airlines to telecoms and consultants, the percentage of service companies in our economies continues to grow. This doesn't even include all the value-added services of those who manufacture physical goods. Chemical companies have come to view their physical product as but one part of an overall inventory control, ordering, delivery, use, and billing service. Computer hardware companies have come to view 24 by 7 service as a basic tool of reliability. Car companies have broadened their vision of the "car-owner economy" to include not only the vehicle but its depreciation, fuel consumption, taxes, workshop service, parts, insurance, and toll charges. Customers can even use computers, appliances, and vehicles on a "pay for service" basis.

Now, your reaction may be, "Still, who needs a text on service strategy and development?" After all, there is a plethora of new product strategy, development, and launch processes and books already available. Again the answer is rather simple. In ways that we shall explain shortly, services are different from products, and despite the growth in services, developing an innovative and sustainable service strategy remains a poorly understood and makeshift process. In this book, we explore how to meet the challenges of competing innovatively through services and thereby developing a clear competitive advantage. Central to the process are three service development activities: (1) service maintenance, (2) improving service performance, and (3) service innovation. In the tradition of the University of Michigan Business School's Management Series, we provide a hands-on approach to developing a service strategy through a process of structuring and implementing these new service development activities. We illustrate the various steps with a variety of case studies and examples that include both traditional retail and service providers, such as IKEA, Ritz-Carlton, and Scandinavian Airline Systems (SAS), and producers of physical goods that have come to differentiate themselves through service development, such as Sterling Pulp Chemicals.

## ■ The Evolution of Services

There is a widespread, naive belief that service development, production, marketing, and management is a simple adaptation of physical goods development, marketing, and management. But don't kid yourself—services are fundamentally different. Whereas physical goods provide a means to an end, services provide the "ends" directly, typically in the form of solutions to customer problems. Consider how physical elements such as foodstuffs and decor provide only the platform of raw materials for a restaurant experience. In a sense, physical products are services waiting to happen. But the restaurant experience itself is a series of linked activities that have the potential to create a differential advantage that is very difficult to copy.

The definition and evolution of services and service production have been central concerns within the "Nordic school" of marketing and quality management.[2] Christian Grönroos established the Nordic school's definition of services and has explored just what makes services and products different. According to Grönroos, "A service is an activity or series of activities of a more or less intangible nature that normally, but not necessarily, take place in interaction between the customer and service employees and/or physical resources or goods and/or systems of the service provider, which are provided as solutions to customer problems."[3]

This definition makes it clear that the production and the consumption of services are very different from the production and consumption of physical goods. Whereas goods are produced in a factory separate from the customer, services are produced in a process that directly involves the customer. The customer is more or less actively involved with the employees, physical resources, and production system of the organization. Let's use this definition to take a closer look at other key differences between services and physical goods.

### Key Differences Between Goods and Services

As solutions to individual customer problems, services are inherently more *heterogeneous* than physical goods. That is, service providers can tailor the service to individual customer needs. As Grönroos's definition emphasizes, the results of a service production process are also more *intangible.* This intangibility makes services inherently more difficult to evaluate. And unlike physical goods, services are often produced (and thereby "consumed") at a time and place of the customer's choosing. This *inseparability* of service production and consumption (a *co-production* with customers) often involves an organization's front-line employees, which means that the service cannot be inventoried and checked for quality assurance. As services are time and place dependent, they are also inherently *perishable.* If the seats on the plane or the rooms in the hotel are not sold, they cannot be stored in inventory. Technology also plays a somewhat different role for services vis-à-vis physical goods. Technology may be embodied in a physical product (such as a computer or digital camera), but from a service perspective, technology may have more to do with allowing customers more input and more control over their lives (as happens with on-line banking or airline booking). We discuss the infusion of technology in services in more detail both later in this chapter and in Chapter Five. Table 1.1 summarizes the key differences between goods and services.

**Table 1.1.** Differences Between Goods and Services

| Goods . . . | Services . . . |
| --- | --- |
| Are a means to an end | Are ends per se (solutions to customer problems or experiences) |
| Are more homogeneous | Are more heterogeneous |
| Are more tangible | Are more intangible |
| Generally separate production and consumption | Are co-produced with customers (production and consumption are inseparable) |
| Are storable (can be inventoried) | Are perishable (can't be inventoried) |
| Embody technology | Use technology to provide customers more control |

Most important from a service improvement and innovation standpoint is that your customers are fellow engineers in the co-production process. Unlike the buyers of physical goods, for whom it is common to translate the "voice of the customer" or external quality into the "voice of the engineer" or internal quality, service customers are intimately involved in the service production process. The implication is that customers can contribute much more to the development of services than they typically can for physical goods. As co-producers or service engineers, customers are an inherently valuable source of new service ideas and innovation. But the value is gained only if you are able to tap your customers' expertise and ideas and translate them into service improvements. This forces us all to know service customers even more intimately than our physical goods customers. Through the Internet, for example, customers are transforming entire business systems as they engage in an active dialogue with companies and each other. This dialogue is increasingly under your customers' control rather than yours. The result is a new marketplace where the customer plays an active role in creating, extracting, and exchanging value. The new service development processes and tools that we describe herein aim to leverage customers as a source of competence for your company.

From an organizational perspective, service production and goods production differ in another important way: *service production is more dependent on your culture and strategy!* Although almost every company today is claiming to be customer focused, relatively few are ready to take the key step of letting customers become the experts in their organizations. Paying close attention to customer needs and accepting the customer into your service design team require a strong customer service culture, one characterized by a passion for delivering high-quality service. This passion is reflected in those companies that put customers' interests, and the front-line employees that serve these interests, first.

## A Goods-to-Services Continuum

Although we contrast goods with services, remember that any given offering is often a combination of the two. Figure 1.1 illustrates how offerings vary along a continuum from pure goods to pure services. It is helpful to consider to which of these four general categories your business belongs. Pure goods producers, such as chemical or food product companies, offer a tangible product that is produced in a factory and packaged or inventoried before the customer gets involved. But as pure goods industries have become low-margin, commodity businesses, this is changing. More and more manufacturers of commodity goods are going down the value chain and developing service offerings to differentiate themselves and build their value propositions. Core goods such as vehicles and data storage systems already contain a significant service component as part of their overall product offering. For vehicle manufacturers, one main goal over the last decade has been to differentiate themselves from competitors on "software" rather than "hardware."[4] Even data hardware suppliers such as IBM and EMC[2] have differentiated themselves over the last decade through their ability to deliver high-quality service to customers.

If you're a core service, such as an airline or Internet service provider (ISP), the service you provide is your main reason for being, be it the on-time arrival of the airline or the connectivity of the ISP. Yet necessary to this core service are significant

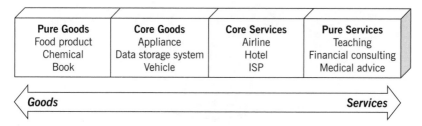

Figure 1.1. The Goods-to-Services Continuum

tangible elements that must be integrated into the service process, such as the food and beverages of an airline or the hardware used to access your ISP. If you are a pure service, such as a teacher or consultant, you offer the most intangible of products. The knowledge or coaching that you offer is consumed as it is produced via direct interaction with the customer.

### Forces Driving the Move Toward Services

What environmental and competitive forces are moving us along the continuum from goods to services? The growth of services is a reflection of fundamental changes in cultures and economies. Consider the four forces illustrated in Figure 1.2. First, individuals simply have less time available to shop and do things on their own as the percentage of working women and single-parent households continues to grow. One result is more meals out, more in-home services, and less time spent shopping for physical goods as a means to an end. Rather, people are more willing to trade time for money to buy services and experiences directly.

A second force is the growing availability of technology that allows customers to perform services themselves when and

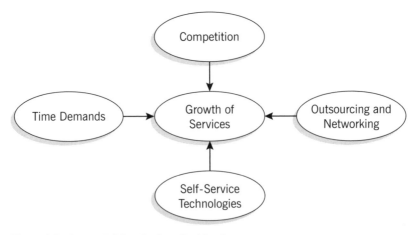

**Figure 1.2.** Factors Driving the Growth of Services

where they can. Paying bills, investing, and shopping on-line and at home are increasingly common ways to cope with the growing complexity of our lives. A third force contributing to our move toward services is a business climate in which organizations are striving to focus on core competencies and, as a result, outsource those services that they cannot cost-effectively provide.

Fourth but not least, the move toward services is a fundamental reaction to the evolution of competition. This competitive evolution, detailed in Figure 1.3, forces companies to evolve over time from competing on product value to competing on service value to competing on solution value, or what we refer to as linked activities. These linked activities are a constellation of related products and services that provide customers with an integrated solution to a particular need or problem. Whether you are selling cake mixes or minivans, as a market matures you eventually find intense competition in every niche of the market. Thus, niches host very similar competitors for whom quality becomes a given and price the main way to compete. This evolution has forced companies to look downstream, or down the value chain, to the possibility of competing for the customer services that surround their products. Rather than sell the cake mix, you bake, frost, and deliver the cake! As you continue to

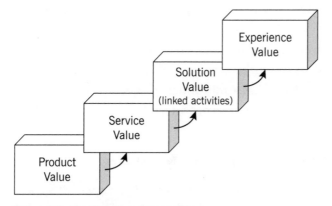

**Figure 1.3.** The Evolution of Competition

develop new services and link them together in your value proposition, these linked activities or service constellations become a critical source of competitive advantage.

In some cases, the evolution of competition drives companies to stage personalized experiences per se and provide experience value.[5] Customers are finding it increasingly cost- and time-effective to pay service providers to "do it for them." Instead of buying the cake mix, frosting and decorating the cake, decorating the house, ordering the pizza, and staging the birthday party, families go to Chuckie Cheese and pay for the whole experience.

It is these services and service constellations and not physical goods that have fueled modern economic growth. There are those who fear that the growth of services is a fundamental threat to our manufacturing base. Indeed, the notion that services cannot survive without a strong manufacturing base is rarely challenged. The more interesting and never-asked question in our minds is, Can manufacturing survive without a strong service base? We think the answer is no! Following the natural evolution of competition illustrated in Figure 1.3, more and more manufacturers must move down the value chain to differentiate themselves and remain profitable. General Electric makes and sells jet engines, but makes more money taking care of them. Thus services break the competitive deadlock of a mature, goods-based economy. As physical goods become more and more a linked part of a constellation of value-added services, solutions, and experiences, the latter subsidizes the former. Just ask yourself the question, Without strong service connections, where will our manufacturing go? Most likely, it will go overseas to a lower-cost producer.

### The Relation of Services to New Technologies

What roles do the infusion of technology, the Internet, and e-commerce play in this development? Technology has become one of the most important parts of a service firm's infrastructure. At Northwest Airlines (NWA), dogged in the past by its low customer satisfaction and service woes, self-service technologies such as e-ticket kiosks and nwa.com have become important sources of customer satisfaction and loyalty. Rated the number one Internet service in the airline industry and one of the top twenty-five websites in the world,[6] nwa.com enhances a customer's overall service experience when and where it is needed.

More generally, and consistent with Figure 1.3, technological advances and e-commerce have become important parts of an integrated solutions concept that provides a constellation of services or an experience per se. Technology cannot entirely replace the human elements of service at such companies as Schwab, Borders, and Disney. In fact, more often than not an effective multichannel strategy that includes e-commerce places even greater service burdens on your organization. Sotheby's, the famous London auction house, has found that for every piece that it sells through its on-line auctions at sothebys.com, it creates five subsequent interactions with front-line service personnel.[7] Although the Sotheby's example may be extreme, the point is simple. *Technology is not a substitute for delivering high-quality service.* Rather, it is an integral part of your service growth and development strategy. Our work with a variety of international companies over the years shows that it's the established service and retail companies, such as NWA and IKEA, that are making the most of their e-commerce activities.

## ■ Evolving Management Thought

Now let's relate our discussion of services and service development to the general evolution of management thought. Consider how your business logic has changed in recent decades. Services are now routinely developed within networks, alliances, and constellations with other companies, organizations, universities, and of course customers. Tore Strandvik, a professor from the Swedish School of Economics and Business Administration in Helsinki, Finland, has developed a useful framework for understanding this evolution. Our variation on his framework is shown in Figure 1.4.[8]

The horizontal axis or strategic focus parallels the evolution of competition depicted in Figure 1.3. The vertical axis captures changes in how we relate to markets and customers over time. We have moved from focusing on individual transactions to focusing on customer contact points or what are often called "moments of truth," to building customer relationships (based on the lifetime value of customers), to building alliances and networks that include customers and even competitors as collaborators. Keep in mind that transactions, moments of truth, and

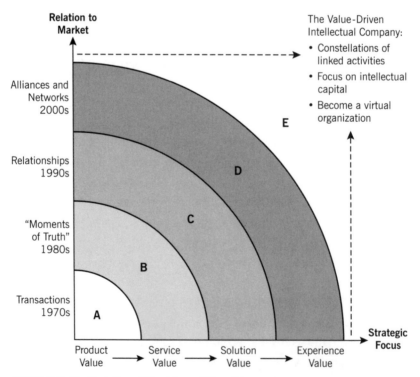

**Figure 1.4.** The Evolution of Management Thought

relationships don't just go away as your organization evolves. As a service organization, you have to become effective at managing individual transactions, service encounters, and customer relationships as you simultaneously build relationships with partners within networks and alliances. One rather obvious implication is that relatively few companies can do it all very well.

Integrating the two axes—Strategic Focus and Relation to Market—results in distinct phases in the evolution of management thought. During phase A, up through the 1970s, the focus was still on product value and individual transactions. The four P's model of marketing (finding the right mix of product, price, promotion, and place or distribution) was the basic model of how to relate to customers and consumers. During phase B, around the 1980s, businesses took much more of a service perspective and focused on total service value within a context of individual service encounters, or moments of truth. What emerged was the notion that services are co-produced with customers in an environment where customization is a plus yet reliability a problem. Essentially, the focus shifted from what was offered to how it was offered and produced.

The transition to phase C coincided with a growing understanding of the lifetime value of customers. Using concepts such as loyalty, one-to-one marketing, customer relationship management (CRM), and customer learning, businesses began to reengineer processes to create satisfied customers, repeat business, positive word of mouth, and greater profits. In our experience, those organizations that have succeeded in creating profitable customer relationships have had something in common: they have developed a unique set of linked activities that provide integrated solutions to customer problems. For example, Southwest Airlines provides point-to-point customers with an inexpensive and convenient alternative to driving, and IKEA provides a unique shopping experience and solutions to the problems of everyday living. In Chapter Two we examine the strategic significance of these linked activities more closely.

Coinciding roughly with the new millennium is the emergence of phase D, within which resources and capabilities are viewed in a broader context of networks and alliances. Here the traditional distinctions separating your company from customers, competitors, and collaborators become weak or fuzzy.[9] As businesses have moved to providing customers with a broader, more integrated experience value, it has become clear that any one organization simply doesn't have the competencies and intellectual capital to do it all. Hence there is strong pressure to share resources and integrate organizations that previously remained at arm's length. For example, SAS cannot fly to every country in the world and support its customers in every airport. So, through Star Alliance, SAS allows customers to make one-stop reservations with multiple airlines, use their alliance partners' lounges and services, and earn frequent-flyer miles. An important implication of phase D is that once-clear branding strategies need to be revisited to better communicate these networks and alliances to an ever changing world.

These phases build up to what Strandvik calls phase E, the development of a value-driven intellectual company. In our adaptation of the framework, excelling at this stage requires your company to focus on three key building blocks. First, identify just what customer problems you are solving and what experiences you plan to provide. In other words, what is your desired constellation of linked activities? Second, focus on building the intellectual capital required. Intellectual capital includes human capital, brand names, culture and values, leadership, and structural capital. By human capital we mean the individual skills, knowledge, creativity, and experience of employees and managers. By structural capital we mean the embodiment, empowerment, and supportive infrastructure of human capital. Third, become a virtual organization. As we'll see, information technology is an essential way to link physically separate organizations as well as organizations and their customers into an effective service constellation.

Let's look at how two companies have used the concepts illustrated in Figure 1.4 to evolve over time. SAS is a traditional service company that competes in an increasingly competitive space; Sterling Pulp Chemicals has used the concepts to evolve from a supplier of commodity chemicals to a provider of linked activities.

## The Transformation at SAS

In years past, the airline business was less complex, and it involved very similar players. In Sweden, SAS enjoyed a monopoly-like situation in which all customers were offered more or less the same service and treated in much the same way. Customers had limited options and, as a result, airlines such as SAS were very hierarchical organizations with multiple layers of management, making them slow to adapt to their changing environment. One of the most profound differences in the airline industry between twenty years ago and now is that today everybody flies! Airlines serve a much wider range of customers with a more diverse set of individual and cultural needs than ever before. One of the first airlines to begin segmenting this diversity and focusing on a particular part of the market was Southwest Airlines. Despite Southwest's success, other airlines have been slow to adapt; they continue to deliver low customer satisfaction as they try to be all things to all people.

SAS has been particularly proactive in understanding how the organization needs to change to remain competitive, including how to adapt its customer options, supplier relations, and organization and management style. In its moves to provide more complete solutions, SAS was one of the first airlines to consider the entire customer experience of traveling and the part that airlines play. Figure 1.5 is a type of learning map that SAS has used to communicate to employees and partners how an airline's moments of truth occur within a broader travel experience.

The travel experience begins when you identify a need to fly; make airport, airline, rent-a-car, and hotel arrangements; and inform colleagues, friends, or family of your plans. Later begins the process of getting to the airport, deciding to check or not check your bags, clearing security, and finding the right gate and lounge. Then there's the flight itself, the rush of

**Air travel is overwhelming**

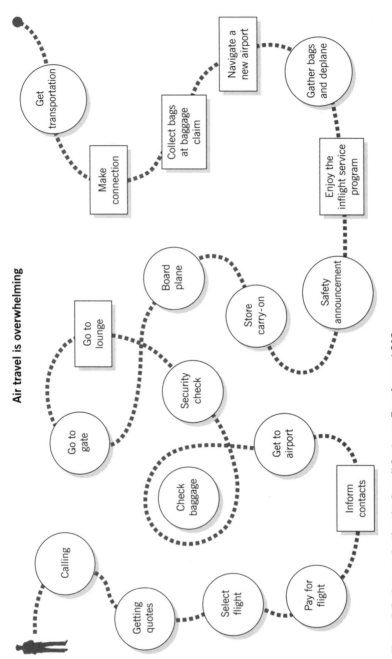

**Figure 1.5. Communicating the Overall Customer Experience at SAS**

in-flight services, bathroom queues, and waiting on the ground for your gate to open. Once on the ground, you still need to navigate the airport, locate and collect your bags, and make further air or ground connections. Even when everything goes right, the result is an overwhelming process of "stopping and starting" that can easily last a whole day. Experienced travelers customize the decisions they make along the way to the airline and airport involved. For example, when you are passing through busy hubs such as Schipol Airport in Amsterdam where connections are tight, checking your bags often results in lost luggage.

Learning maps like the one in Figure 1.5 have helped SAS understand that air travel is more than just a couple of hours in the air. Customers have individual needs and concerns. They bring their preflight experiences (the rush-hour traffic or rude counter agent) and postflight fears (Will I make my connection? Will my bags be there?) on the plane with them.

SAS has used its understanding of the overall customer experience and the linked activities involved to improve its customers' experience and the company's approach to management. As other airlines continue to struggle to provide the basics, SAS succeeds in meeting more individual-level needs through service development. In subsequent chapters, we'll show you how, for example, SAS is tailoring its food service operations by including the customer in the process. The challenge is to continue to remove barriers to product and service variation so that customers can design and tailor their own travel experience. Attempting to meet this challenge requires SAS to develop a thorough knowledge and understanding of its customers' needs and preferences. This knowledge of the customer, in turn, affects SAS's relationships with its employees and suppliers. As a result of studying its customers' experiences, SAS has developed a much better understanding of its own core competencies and limitations. Guided by these insights, SAS relies increasingly on suppliers to invent and deliver superior value to customers. Through outsourcing and networking, different companies' competencies are combined to deliver a superior customer experience.

The effect on senior management is that executives have either had to change or be replaced to help SAS grow the necessary intellectual capital and become a knowledge organization. Executives have also adopted an "inverted pyramid" approach to management. In a traditional organizational hierarchy or pyramid, senior executives focus on controlling an organization in a top-down fashion. An inverted pyramid approach recognizes that executives and managers serve in more of a support capacity for those employees who interact directly with customers. Rather than dictate what people should do, senior executives at SAS provide front-line service personnel with the information and resources needed to support customers throughout the travel process. Improved customer information technology and employee training are central to an SAS service system in which employees make sure that customers have a pleasant, pain-free, and cost-effective travel experience. By empowering employees to satisfy customers and recover dissatisfied customers, and by empowering customers to take more control over routine tasks such as food service, SAS has continued to adapt.

## The Transformation at Sterling Pulp Chemicals

Now consider a physical goods manufacturer that has evolved and transformed itself not just into a service provider but into the provider of integrated solutions. Sterling Pulp Chemicals (SPC) is a division of Sterling Chemicals, headquartered in Toronto, Canada. Like many suppliers, SPC found itself in price wars selling commodity products to customers in the paper products industry. SPC emerged from these wars by transforming itself from a chemical supplier into a service and solutions provider. One of its first steps was to conduct a series of interviews with key customers regarding their core business. The purpose of the interviews was to gain a deep understanding of customers' entire operations and how they order, ship, use, mix, and dispose of SPC's chemicals in the process. This understanding allowed SPC to recognize what customers would rather not be doing and thus recognize potential areas in which to develop value-added services.

With this knowledge, SPC began to explore service development options at its customers' mill sites. Examined were interfaces with customers' operations (physically, how did the plants operate), chemical usage (efficiencies), and distribution. The project teams included management, line-level workers, their union representatives, and key customers. SPC identified four service development options: (1) offer "over the fence" production and supply, (2) provide technical expertise to optimize chemical usage, (3) enter marketing agreements with other producers to bundle complementary products, and (4) improve distribution and related services through a significant investment in information technology.

SPC subsequently implemented a series of continuous improvements to its distribution-related services using input from key customers. It became an industry pioneer in instituting on-line ordering and a railcar tracking system to help customers locate just where the products are at a point in time. This resulted in more efficient production scheduling at customers' facilities. Integration of the inventory management and rail fleet management systems further allowed customers to reduce both the cost and number of transactions performed at the pulp mills. Using SPC's open Intranet-based database, customers can access, add to, or modify order, tracking, and lab-related information.

Figure 1.6 illustrates the integrated system that SPC offers its customers. A Microsoft SQL server provides different service solutions to participating customers. Through the system, customers access the on-line

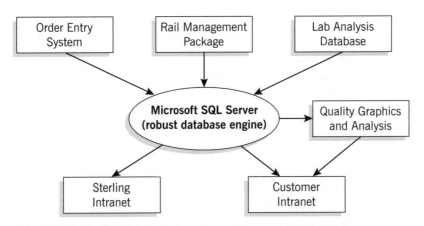

**Figure 1.6.** SPC's Fully Integrated Distribution–Customer Service IT System

order entry system, the rail management and tracking system, and technical expertise through a lab analysis database. The database engine makes the information available within both SPC (via Sterling intranet) and the customers' operations (via customer intranet). Over time, customers use multiple, coordinated services to do more than just acquire a particular chemical for a production process. They develop more efficient production schedules and chemical usage. SPC builds a symbiotic relationship with its customers in which both parties become irreplaceable. The changes at Sterling Pulp have resulted in a service system of linked activities that provide customers over-the-fence service and supply even when company and customer are thousands of miles apart.

But the changes did not come quickly. SPC had to adapt its culture and develop new core competencies. To do so, Sterling's management team employed an explicit process called customer policy deployment.[10] First was the move to a customer-focused mission and vision statement: "Sterling Pulp Chemical's vision is to be the best supplier of products and service that meet the existing and future needs of our customers." New to the mission statement was the emphasis on service and future needs. Second was the establishment of explicit and measurable goals for growth that would come from doing more business with existing customers. Third was a communication strategy that emphasized a culture of openness with respect to information, especially cost information up and down different levels of the organization and with customers. A key to the culture change was the retention and hiring of people who bought into the mission and vision. Finally, the process had to be aligned. For this purpose, SPC developed a set of detailed action plans and project teams (management, line-level workers, and key customers) to implement the strategy.

As a result of these changes, SPC now operates as a price leader. By building trust relationships and providing integrated solutions, SPC has enabled its customers to significantly reduce both freight costs and total average costs, and opened windows for further service development. In addition, the economies of scale that SPC has achieved through its ordering and transportation system have created a channel of distribution through which it bundles and ships competitors' products. Thus, as SPC moves to phases D and E in the framework, the distinction between customers, competitors, and collaborators continues to blur.

# ■ From Dream to Reality

Unfortunately, service success stories have been more the exception than the rule of late. Not all is well in the service economy: customer satisfaction with services has generally declined over the past decade. The American Customer Satisfaction Index (ACSI), developed by Claes Fornell, the second author, and colleagues at the University of Michigan Business School,[11] measures satisfaction and other performance benchmarks for products, services, and government agencies across the U.S. economy. Satisfaction is reported using a 100-point index of satisfaction survey measures. Figure 1.7 shows changes in ACSI scores for five major service sectors in the economy.[12]

The general decline in service satisfaction is likely due to multiple factors. As mentioned in our discussion of the airline industry, the service customer base grew and became more heterogeneous throughout the 1990s, which made customer satisfaction more difficult to achieve. Another contributing factor is the use of CRM systems that channel resources toward a smaller group of highly profitable customers and away from what is

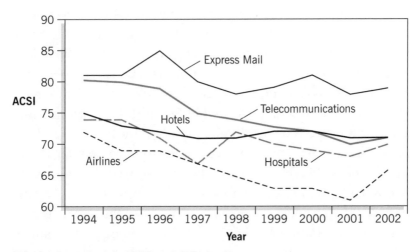

**Figure 1.7.** Changes in ACSI Service Satisfaction

often a much larger group of increasingly dissatisfied customers. And as the U.S. and other economies prospered throughout the 1990s, the general decline in the unemployment rate also made it more and more difficult to find and keep good service employees. Satisfaction rose significantly in the past year for airline travelers, but largely because relatively few people were flying after September 11, 2001. Recent increases in other ACSI service industries are encouraging. But your strategy simply can't be to wait for an increase in unemployment to fix the problem. The best way to create a more satisfied and profitable customer base is to implement a service strategy that leverages service maintenance, improvement, and innovation.

## ■ The Plan of the Book

Our overriding goal throughout the book will be to bring structure to what has been a very ad hoc, unstructured process of service development. In Chapter Two we explore the basis of a competitive service advantage and how to create one. Excellent service companies use a continuous process of building a culture, staying focused on a particular market or market segment, and linking multiple activities to solve customer problems or provide unique experiences. Linking activities into a seamless system requires that you focus on three related service development processes. We refer to these processes as the hierarchy of service development, illustrated in Figure 1.8. Chapters Three through Five focus on the different levels of the hierarchy. At the base is service maintenance, which is the topic of Chapter Three. The theme of this chapter is that, because services are inherently less reliable than physical goods, it is essential to begin by removing "things gone wrong." In the middle of the hierarchy and the topic of Chapter Four is improving service performance, which involves improving customer satisfaction and loyalty

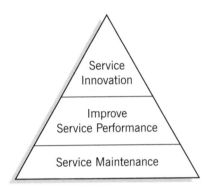

**Figure 1.8.** The Hierarchy of Service Development

through customization of the service offering to market segment or individual-level customer needs. Chapter Five focuses on the top of the hierarchy, service innovation. This chapter takes a particular look at the role of customers themselves in helping you generate and develop innovative solutions to customer problems. Our final chapter, Chapter Six, looks across the frameworks, cases, and examples used throughout the book to identify lessons for service leaders.

**CHAPTER SUMMARY**

Don't expect the service economy to go away. Expect it to grow and become more complex as service alliances and networks continue to evolve and businesses move beyond physical goods to deliver more services, solutions, and experiences. Foremost you should recognize that services are different! The strategies and ways of competing that may have worked in the past won't necessarily work in these new competitive spaces. As solutions to customer problems, services are more heterogeneous, intangible, and perishable than physical goods. Co-produced directly with customers, services offer the advantage of customization and the prospect that something is likely to go wrong.

The frameworks and case examples throughout the book are designed to help you prosper amidst these challenges. Our framework for building a competitive service advantage focuses on building a customer service culture; staying focused on particular customers; and linking activities to create integrated customer solutions, superior service experiences, and more profitable relationships. We accomplish these goals through the implementation of a service development hierarchy that involves removing things gone wrong, improving service performance, and service innovation.

### Questions for Consideration

1. Objectively, where is your organization today on the goods-to-services continuum? Is this position consistent with how managers, employees, and customers perceive the organization?
2. What forces are driving your organization along the good-to-services continuum to become either more or less service oriented?

**2**

# Creating a
# Service Advantage

Service maintenance, improvement, and innovation are the building blocks that your company needs to compete effectively in a service economy. As when building a house or an airplane, you must have a strategy and plan in order to use these building blocks. What are the strategic goals of your service development? How should you go about achieving these goals? Put simply, what is your overall strategy for creating a competitive service advantage? Here in Chapter Two we take a closer look at the foundations of this strategy. We develop a framework for creating a competitive service advantage that involves building an organizational and customer service culture, staying focused on a particular customer population or market

25

segment, and linking service activities to form a seamless system. After using the "IKEA Saga" to illustrate our framework in action, we develop a set of dimensions for evaluating the opportunities that exist for building a service advantage. These dimensions include a thorough understanding of your cultural evolution, service evolution, and customer relationship evolution.

### ■ How to Create a Service Advantage

Figure 2.1 uses a Venn diagram to illustrate the strategic positions of your company, your customers, and your competition as you attempt to create a service advantage. The three circles in the figure represent your customers' needs, what your company has to offer customers, and what your competitor has to offer customers.[1] Consider first those areas where either two or three circles overlap. Customer needs that are provided by both you and

**Figure 2.1.** Your Customers, Your Competitors, Your Company

the competition are considered basics. Although these needs are important to customers in a general sense, they fail to differentiate between two competitors. We refer to them as basics because customers come to expect these aspects as givens across competitors. Customers come to take them more or less for granted, be they the safety of an airline or the reliability of ATMs.

In contrast, those customer needs that you provide but competitors do not are your source of competitive advantage. They are the reasons why your customers choose you over competitors. Likewise, customer needs that are uniquely met by your competitors are their relative advantage and your competitive vulnerability. When customers switch to a competitor, these are usually the reasons why. Qualities that both you and your competition provide that don't match customers' needs are also interesting. We often see service as well as product companies copying what competitors do without ever checking to see if it is something customers even need or want. A study by one of the authors found, for example, that competitive benchmarking on "best in class" performance can cause companies to lose customer focus.[2] Resources tied up in these products, services, or activities are candidates for reallocation.

Now consider those parts of the circles that don't overlap. If you can recognize them, customer needs not currently provided for are opportunities for you to move first and create a competitive advantage. Those areas where either you or your competitor are providing things that customers don't currently use or want are additional candidates for possible reallocation, unless there is reason to believe that customer needs are moving toward them. This is why it makes sense to monitor competitors' activities but not necessarily copy them.

So how do you take advantage of market opportunities to move first and create a competitive service advantage? Be it with Disney, Southwest Airlines, or IKEA, our experience with a variety of service and retail companies reveals basic similarities among those who excel at this process. The first similarity is a strong company culture. Even with the influx of technology in our society, service is still primarily about people. And service people require a positive corporate and customer service culture. The second similarity is a clear and consistent focus on a market segment. The third similarity is that this culture and focus leverage the organization's ability to link activities or create a constellation of services that provide unique solutions to customer needs. At Disney this linkage is embodied in the Disney "orbit." As we describe in more detail later in the chapter, Disney's orbit focuses on delivering the highest-quality booking, lodging, theme park, dining, and entertainment experiences possible.[3] At Southwest Airlines the linkage centers on providing the most cost-effective and reliable point-to-point travel experience possible. At IKEA, to which we pay special attention here in Chapter Two, linked activities are all about making everyday life better for the "many people" not served by more expensive stores. The constant process of building the culture, staying focused, and linking activities is illustrated in Figure 2.2.

### Build the Culture

Service excellence begins and ends with the culture. We distinguish two levels of culture: a general organizational culture and a more specific customer service culture.[4] Organizational culture is your set of more or less common values, beliefs, and norms. Your organization must value or believe that certain ways of doing business, such as treating employees with respect and building customer relationships, are critical to long-run performance. In *The Soul of Service*, Leonard Berry identifies seven commonly held values that sustain excellent service organizations: innovation, excellence, joy, teamwork, respect, integrity, and social profit. These core values are described in Table 2.1.[5]

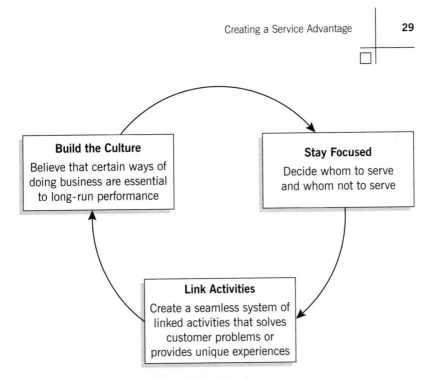

**Figure 2.2.** Building a Competitive Service Advantage

**Table 2.1.** Berry's Core Values That Sustain Service Performance

| Core Value | Description |
| --- | --- |
| Innovation | Challenge the status quo to produce something better. |
| Excellence | Don't settle for "good," because good isn't good enough. |
| Joy | Create a joyful, fun place to work. |
| Teamwork | Recognize that being a member of a tested, challenged, and successful team is as important in work as in life. |
| Respect | Respect your employees, customers, partners, and business community. |
| Integrity | Value honesty and integrity as the right way and the best way to compete. |
| Social profit | Produce benefits to society beyond narrow, economic goals. Enrich all of your stakeholders in society. |

Whereas your service strategy and tactics may evolve and adapt over time, your organization's value system (its "soul," so to speak) remains relatively stable. Take some time to reflect on just how well your organization embraces each of these values.

Your organization's soul manifests or reflects itself every day through organizational norms or ways of doing business. When a Wal-Mart sales associate experiments with displays at the point of purchase, he or she reflects the value that Wal-Mart places on innovation. When the same associate helps communicate and transfer his or her ideas to other associates or stores, the act reflects the value that Wal-Mart places on teamwork. It is these values, Berry argues, that help an organization's leadership articulate its "reason for being." As an enabler, you should devote considerable time and effort to communicating these core values in the workplace, not through memos or e-mails but through interacting with your people and leading by example.

Your organization's core values provide a basis for developing a more specific customer service culture. Whereas the organizational culture embodies reasons for being, the customer service culture is a more instrumental understanding of the business model that allows the organization to generate resources, prosper, and grow. One prominent example of a customer service culture as a business or profit model is the "service-profit chain."[6] Hotel executive J. W. Marriott Jr. describes the logic of the service-profit chain very simply: "My father knew that if he had happy employees, he would have happy customers, and then that would result in a good bottom line."[7] Your culture and philosophy are the basis of your service management system. Beyond the corporate or organizational values shown in Table 2.1, the more specific customer service culture underscores the need to invest in employees who can deliver excellent customer service and in customers who never have a reason to do business with anyone else. The resulting profits provide resources for reinvesting in the organization to ensure long-run success.

At the heart of the customer service culture is the belief that the culture that customers experience is the culture that employees experience. It recognizes that service is a process or system within which customers and employees work together. For a customer service culture to emerge, all the elements of the system must work and function together smoothly and seamlessly.[8] Overall the system must make cultural and economic sense to those working within it. To produce a smooth, seamless system, employees must operate in a positive work environment in which both they and customers are highly valued and respected. Employees must understand the central role they play in determining a company's performance. And they need the freedom to act as they see fit. At Southwest Airlines, Herb Kelleher has always put his employees first. One of his mottoes is never to sacrifice an employee, or let an employee be mistreated, for the sake of a customer. It's not that customers are unimportant— Southwest remains an industry leader in customer satisfaction.[9] Rather, Southwest's underlying service culture of respecting and rewarding employees is the first step in Southwest's employee-customer-profit chain.

### Stay Focused on Your Market Segment

Building and maintaining a service advantage requires market segmentation. Your ability to build the culture and subsequently link activities depends on remaining strategically focused on a particular customer population.[10] Deciding whom to serve and whom not to serve is essential, or the "seams" in the system will rupture. IKEA's service concept and activities are, for example, explicitly aimed at avoiding the wealthier people in society who are served by higher-end furniture stores. They focus on the "many people" who want contemporary, reasonably priced furniture and are willing to participate in the process. Low-cost manufacturing and customer participation (through the use of informative catalogues, websites and displays, and self-transport and self-assembly of the furniture) are essential to IKEA's service concept and strategy. Other companies focus on very different segments. The focus at Southwest Airlines is on the point-to-point travel customer who might use other means of transport; Ritz-Carlton focuses on the luxury, service-intensive hotel customer.

The key is to avoid stretching your culture and the linked activities you have forged in an attempt to serve too many different types of customers. Otherwise the system breaks down and the advantage is lost. If IKEA employees were asked to perform services for high-end customers that the "many people" are willing to do themselves, this request would be inconsistent with the entire business model that Ingvar Kamprad and his successors have built up over decades. If Ritz-Carlton employees were overwhelmed with performing routine tasks for the masses, their actions would be inconsistent with the highly personalized service that Ritz employees provide to a select segment of customers. The value that the Ritz places on employees as "ladies and gentlemen serving ladies and gentlemen" would be undermined.

### Link Activities

In the world of physical goods, competitors may use either segmentation or differentiation to compete.[11] As described in the previous section, segmentation involves focusing on a subset of the market, or market segment, to better serve the needs of that segment. For example, a low-fat food product is designed and developed to meet the needs of a more health conscious customer. Differentiation involves making a product different or better in some way to appeal to customers, such as a food product that tastes better than competing products. What makes the service context fundamentally different from a physical goods context is that segmentation and differentiation are more inherently intertwined. As captured in our framework, creating a service advantage requires both! Successful service companies combine segmentation and differentiation as part of their seamless system of linked activities. It is the linked activities that provide the differentiation.

Linked activities may be viewed from different perspectives, two of which we illustrate here. Walt Disney World's "customer orbit," illustrated in Figure 2.3, looks at linked activities from the standpoint of a customer's purchase-consumption-repurchase cycle.[12] Managers and employees of Walt Disney World use the orbit to understand the co-production between customers and employees, improve customers' overall experience, and identify opportunities to grow. Each stage in the orbit can be viewed as a category of activities that, when linked, provide a powerful customer experience.

**Figure 2.3. Disney's Customer Orbit**

The process begins when customers are attracted to a Disney theme park or resort. Employees responding to customer inquiries must be able to explain which attractions and resorts are best for which customers and adapt the offering to a customer's budget constraints, which results in a customer booking. The consumption phase of the process begins upon arrival, when Disney ensures that customers start off on the right foot. This includes a massive bus and parking system that continuously ferries customers to and from Disney attractions, which are the heart of the Disney consumption experience. Figure 2.3 describes the attractions as theme parks and resorts, the latter of which also have their own themes. These are the places where customers experience the enjoyment of interacting with Disney's characters, cast, attractions, and accommodations. As with arrival, customer departure is designed to be as friendly, smooth, and pleasant as possible. Finally, the orbit recognizes the power of satisfied customers to recommend Walt Disney World to others. By linking each category of activities together into a seamless system, Disney creates multiple opportunities to repeat the cycle through attraction of the same customers or referrals, be it for family trips, reunions, weddings, or business conferences.

Linked activities at IKEA, the Swedish-based international furniture retailer, are illustrated by the activities "map" in Figure 2.4.[13] The larger ovals distinguish the higher-order themes that are central to IKEA's strategy, including modular furniture design, self-service and self-selection by customers, and low-cost manufacturing. These higher-order themes are identified and implemented through various linked activities. The activities represent the more concrete norms or operating policies by which the themes are implemented. For example, the combined activities of self-assembly, in-house design, "knock-down" packaging, ease of assembly, and a wide product variety achieve the modular design that is a central part of IKEA's strategy.

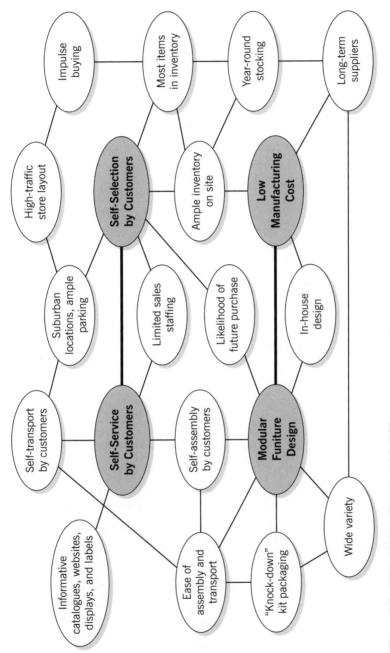

**Figure 2.4.  IKEA's Strategy Themes and Activities**

As our framework in Figure 2.2 shows, linking activities into a seamless system requires both a strong cultural and market focus. Notice that the lower part of IKEA's linked-activities map focuses on internal activities (*modular furniture design* and *low-cost manufacturing*). These internal activities support the more external or customer process activities that dominate the top half of the figure. (*Self-service by customers* captures those activities by which customers learn about, transport, and assemble products themselves, and *self-selection by customers* captures the customer's role in taking products directly out of an open warehouse.) Everyone at IKEA must understand how the values, norms, and expectations of its culture support these linked activities, which form the basis of the company's business model. IKEA's culture, referred to as "the IKEA way," emphasizes thrift, inventiveness, and hard work and is strongly influenced by its founder and spiritual leader, Ingvar Kamprad. This culture remains focused on providing the "many people" with contemporary and affordable furniture and furnishings. In the next section of this chapter, we explore the evolution of IKEA's culture, strategy, and market segmentation in more detail.

*The source of advantage in linked activities lies in the difficulty that any competitor has in replicating an entire system once established!* For example, a competitor may be able to replicate any one activity or small set of activities that a Disney or IKEA perform well, but replicating an entire system of linked activities that grows and becomes stronger over time is extremely hard. IKEA's "map" contains sixteen activities linked to four strategic themes. Suppose for simplicity that the likelihood of a competitor's coming into a market and successfully replicating any one of these activities were as high as 80 percent over a given period of time. Over that same period of time, the probability of replicating the entire system would be 0.80 multiplied sixteen times, or about 2.8 percent. Now you can see why it has been so difficult for competitors to copy service leaders—the advantage is real.

## ■ The IKEA Saga

IKEA is an excellent example of an organization that has built a strong culture, remained focused on its market segment, and successfully linked activities over time to create a sustainable competitive advantage. Let's look at how IKEA's culture, strategy, and activities have evolved over time, referred to in the Nordic tradition as the IKEA Saga.[14] The story illustrates the continuous process of building the culture, staying focused, and constantly linking activities. (We encourage you to read the excerpt from Bo Edvardsson and Bo Enquist's recent article on the IKEA Saga, which appears in the Appendix.)

IKEA's roots are in the Småland, a poor and harsh region in southern Sweden. It was here that the company's founder, Ingvar Kamprad, was born in 1926 on a farm in the village of Agunnaryd near Älmhult, where IKEA's product development, quality control, catalogue production, and the central warehouse for Northern Europe are still located. Growing up in the Småland, Kamprad came to value thrift, inventiveness, simplicity, humility, hard work, willingness to accept responsibility, leading by example, and a strong sense of togetherness and enthusiasm. IKEA was built on and continues to embrace these values. Today's employees and managers are part of the "IKEA family," an extension of Kamprad's original staffing concept that included only family members and neighbors.

Furniture entered IKEA's product line in 1948 for the first time, after which IKEA began selling mail-order furniture at factory prices. Following Kamprad's decision to sell through the mail, there was significant fallout from large, established furniture companies. Suppliers who chose to do business with IKEA were threatened with boycotts, and "IKEA was literally thrown out of the bid furniture trade fair in Stockholm."[15] But orders continued to pour in, and IKEA found ways to turn problems into opportunities. Kamprad needed a way to educate customers so they could learn about and see the furniture for themselves and understand differences in quality at different price levels. The result was a "shabby building in Älmhult." As he describes,

> In the autumn of 1952 we completed the catalogue, which came out in time for the opening of the furniture exhibition on March 18, 1953. . . . We displayed our furniture on two levels [at two levels of quality]. We could now at last show those cheap ironing boards alongside those that cost five kronor more and were of good quality. And people did just what we had hoped; they wisely chose the more expensive ironing board. At that moment, the basis of the modern IKEA concept was created, and in principle still applies. First and foremost, use a catalogue to tempt people to come to an exhibition, which today is our store.[16]

Necessity has been the mother of invention. Today IKEA makes creative use of inventories, displays, catalogues, and websites to educate and serve customers in a cost-effective way. Involving customers in the process became a major part of the strategy. Self-service and self-selection by customers allow IKEA to sell good-quality furniture at the lowest possible prices and focus on creating knowledgeable employees and providing childcare, restaurant, product return, and other services. To avoid the boycotts back in the 1950s, IKEA began designing its own furniture and, in the process, came across the concept of self-assembled furniture. Kamprad tells the story of packing up a table after photographing it for the catalogue. Gilles Lundgren, a young draftsman from the ad agency, muttered something like, "God, what a lot of space it takes up. Let's take the legs off and put them under the tabletop."[17] This was IKEA's first flat parcel, which ultimately yielded the modular furniture and self-assembly concepts that are integral to its linked activities. By involving the customer in self-assembly and self-transport, IKEA could use its savings on shipping and inventory costs to provide a higher-quality product for the price.

Notice the linkages created in Figure 2.4 among the informative displays, ample inventory, and strategic emphasis on self-service and self-selection by customers. These linkages extend to the innovative approach that IKEA has taken to keeping its manufacturing costs low. Recall that in 1955, after facing boycotts from designers, IKEA began designing its own furniture. Not only did it leverage Kamprad's emphasis on inventiveness and thrift, it turned a disadvantage into another advantage. Manufacturing costs were kept low through long-term relationships with suppliers. By the early 1960s, as IKEA started to grow internationally, it was faced with a need for production capacity outside Sweden. Kamprad turned to Poland, then a communist country. Initially appalled by the conditions, Kamprad took a long-term approach to changing them:

"At first we did a bit of advance smuggling. Illegally, we took tools such as files, spare parts for machines, and even carbon [ribbons and paper] for ancient typewriters. . . . We bought nose and mouth protectors when we saw the dreadful environment, and we took a whole lot of second-hand machines from a firm in Jönköping and installed them in Poland instead. . . . Slowly and with repeated reverses, we helped to build up a modern furniture industry."[18]

Kamprad's success in Poland is directly related to the company's values and culture. Beyond the surface of the environment and the politics, Kamprad saw a people who shared the same values as the Smålanders—an emphasis on thrift, inventiveness, and hard work.

What has allowed IKEA to leverage its linked activities and the culture on which they are built is its focus and commitment to serving the "many rather than the few." Targeting the many is a way to serve society. But as these customers don't have the same monetary resources as the "few," IKEA must be much cheaper. So IKEA strives to sell items that are astonishingly cheap for the quality and to avoid items found in upper-class stores:

"Standing on the side of the majority of people means representing the interests of ordinary people, no matter whether that is good or bad for our own, short-term interests. It means getting rid of designs which are difficult and expensive to produce, even if they are easy to sell."[19]

IKEA believes in creating a better life for the majority of the people who do not have the majority of the money. It has decided whom to serve and whom not to serve. In keeping with Berry's values (as shown in Table 2.1), IKEA also has a larger social mission that it takes very seriously. Around the world, a disproportionately large portion of resources is used to satisfy a relatively small part of the population. By saying no to many new and beautifully designed products, IKEA hopes to change the situation. In doing so, it has entrenched itself by serving an underserved market.

As IKEA has grown and opened stores around the world, it has always asked the question, How do we protect the culture, or what has come to be called the IKEA way? One key is to grow slowly and deliberately, allowing the culture to take hold on a local level and find the people who buy into the values and norms. Sometimes the road is bumpy, much like the roads in the Småland. It took time for IKEA to understand the differences and culture clashes between Europe and North America. But in an age when many retailers open and close hundreds of stores every year, IKEA grows slowly, deliberately, and profitably.

Another key is IKEA's focus on employees—valuing their input and innovativeness, delegating responsibility, and promoting teamwork to achieve a common goal. On IKEA Day, which takes place once a year, IKEA invites all employees to come to work for free. In exchange, those employees share all the revenues that pass through the store on that day. IKEA Day not only shares the wealth with employees but also creates an enthusiasm that few firms can match.

## ■ The Hierarchy of Service Development

Obviously not every company is a Disney or IKEA. However, we believe that the process of building the culture, staying focused, and linking activities applies to all companies seeking to build a competitive service advantage. Some are simply much better at it than others. Of course, organizations begin at very different starting points. Our hierarchy of service development, introduced in Chapter One and shown in Figure 1.8, provides a basis for understanding where you need to start.

The foundation of the hierarchy is service maintenance. Just getting the basics right can be a daunting task for those operating in very complex systems or environments, such as air travel, in which there are a lot of variables not under direct control. Ticket agents, gate agents, pilots, and flight attendants have little or no control over a host of factors that adversely affect their ability to deliver quality service, from the performance of other airlines and the behavior of passengers to the weather. In Chapter Three we describe how such methods as service process mapping help you identify failure points in service systems and develop solutions. Your service must be reliable and capable of providing the basics, where the focus is on eliminating "things gone wrong" as opposed to improving "things gone right." You have to perform well at this level to move up the hierarchy.

Once you do well on the basics, you can afford to allocate more resources to move up the hierarchy and improve service performance. As detailed in Chapter Four, this requires formal research to identify the drivers of satisfaction and loyalty and how well you perform on them according to your customers. IKEA's linked activities provide customers with a variety of benefits, from the in-store experience and convenience to perceived value. For IKEA the question is, In just what areas that have a large impact on customer satisfaction and loyalty is the company performing relatively poorly according to customers? Improving service performance is a process of identifying these benefits, allocating resources, and improving them.

At the top of the hierarchy, companies seek more radical service innovations, which is the focus of Chapter Five. Organizations operating at this level include those for which service innovation is necessary in order to sustain demand. In the entertainment industry, for example, Disney does an excellent job of paying constant attention to all three levels in the hierarchy. Disney emphasizes cost-effective implementation and continuous improvements in all of its theme parks and resorts. But what feeds demand for the theme parks and resorts is innovation in the form of new movies and the characters they develop.[20] Organizations attempting to transition from one level of competition to another (see Figure 1.3 in Chapter One), such as by moving from delivering product value to delivering service value, are also candidates for service innovation. A good example is SPC, whose case we looked at in Chapter One. SPC built on its core chemical product offerings to develop completely new competencies as a service and solutions provider.

Our hierarchy of service development is aimed at meeting a corresponding hierarchy of customers' needs. Consider the hierarchy of passenger needs for SAS shown in Figure 2.5. SAS's customer research reveals a clear hierarchy that starts with the need to "get us there safely." The interesting thing about these service basics is that as long as they are provided, they go unnoticed. They are simply expected to be there. They have no particular capability to create satisfied and loyal customers because they are expected! But once you fail to provide them, they have a huge capacity to create dissatisfaction and customer defection. As the events of September 11, 2001, demonstrated to all airlines and their passengers, the basics can never be taken for granted. In the case of SAS, the basics include safety, reliability, convenience, and "getting us there on time."

**Figure 2.5.** The SAS Hierarchy of Passenger Needs

As SAS moves up in the hierarchy, it continuously improves its services (be they ticketing or serving meals) to the levels of "help us [customers] through the process" and "support what we [customers] need or want to do." These "things gone right" help the company increase satisfaction and subsequent loyalty. Whereas failing on the basics would cause customers to eliminate you from their consideration set, improving service performance gives customers a reason to choose you over competitors. Finally, innovation at SAS is about providing highly individualized services to support a customer's own situation through a combination of self-service technology and personal service. Customer relationship management (CRM) systems are proving particularly valuable as a way to help service providers understand an individual customer's history and preferences and personalize the service experience. Service innovations can become higher-order themes in your seamless system of linked activities, just as modular furniture design became a part of IKEA's strategy. If you develop these themes before your competitors and successfully link them to existing service activities, you can create customers for life.

## ■ Where to Start?

Choosing just what combination of service maintenance, improvement, and innovation is right for your organization depends on three critical dimensions: your stages of service evolution, cultural evolution, and customer evolution. Whereas service evolution refers to the types of opportunities available, cultural and customer evolution refer to your ability to make good on these opportunities. Let's describe each dimension in turn.

### How Evolved Is Your Service Offering?

In other words, where is your organization on the goods-to-services continuum discussed in Chapter One (see Figure 1.1)? Do you provide primarily a tangible good or a complete solution? Consider three companies at different stages of service evolution: a goods company, a single-service company, and a solutions company (a supplier of multiple, linked service activities). For the goods company, the opportunities to innovate through services are wide open. Increasingly companies are moving "downstream" as a way to differentiate through service development.[21] Such a movement requires understanding the entire life cycle use of a physical good beyond its initial purchase, including its application, financing, upkeep, insurance, resale, and so on. As mentioned earlier, General Electric makes more money maintaining jet engines than selling them. The challenge for goods companies is to understand just what service competencies and capabilities to create.

For the service company, the opportunity is to improve service performance or innovate by linking more than one service together, as when SAS links airline service with hotel service (through Radisson SAS). For the solutions company, the options for innovation are different. For a company like IKEA that has already developed solutions for everyday living, growth comes primarily through increasing its share of an existing market (through increased satisfaction and loyalty) or geographical expansion (building the culture, linking the activities, and staying focused in a new location).

### How Evolved Is Your Culture?

Is your organizational culture capable of supporting a customer-focused service strategy? Cultural evolution is a necessary condition for moving up in the hierarchy of service development. Although SPC had to create whole new service capabilities, it was working from a position of strength with respect to its culture. To build its new service capabilities, SPC built on a strong culture of commitment to total quality management and innovation in its core chemical businesses. Disney's ability to maintain the level of innovation it requires is also highly dependent on its ability to maintain a creative culture.

For companies with weak or even negative cultures, the options are narrower. Until the culture improves and grows, all of the company's energy is consumed just getting the basics right. Continental Airlines is a great example.[22] Just a decade ago, Continental was on the verge of bankruptcy, for the third time! The culture was so bad that Continental employees ripped the insignia off their uniforms because they were embarrassed to let people know where they worked. CEO Gordon Bethune hired all new senior executives to build a new culture. But from a quality improvement standpoint, the implications of Continental's predicament were clear—focus on improving the basics!

That meant getting customers there on time, reliably, with their luggage. Only after they started getting the basics right could Continental focus on delivering world-class service. They had to start linking activities at the bottom of the hierarchy of customer needs before adding links going up the hierarchy. Anyone who has flown Continental over the last decade can't help but be impressed by the transformation.

### How Evolved Are Your Customer Relationships?

As will become clear in subsequent chapters, innovation in a service context requires close cooperation with customers. When you're getting the basics wrong, everybody knows it. You don't need customers to tell you. But in their role as co-producers and engineers in the co-production process, service customers are one of your best sources of both information and innovation. The question is whether you have the kind of relationship with customers necessary to move from merely being acquainted to becoming partners in a service development process. Partnering with customers means sharing resources as well as information. It is no coincidence that when SPC made its transition from a goods company to an IT-based service provider, it worked intimately with a handful of its closest customers.

### CHAPTER SUMMARY

Like building anything else, building a competitive service advantage requires a strategy and plan. Our argument is that excellent service companies pursue a common strategy: build the culture, stay focused, and link activities. Less common is an organization's ability to stay with this strategy and make it work. Strong service cultures embrace values that support certain ways of both doing business and generating a profit. Service is about people serving people, and service people need to work in an environment in which they are highly valued. Leveraging and maintaining your culture require a consistency of purpose and focus through market segmentation. Ultimately it's the linked activities, or seamless system in which employees and customers interact, that provide the differentiation.

Just where any individual company or organization starts linking activities depends on its stages of service, cultural, and customer relationship evolution. Taken together, these evolutionary dimensions provide direction for implementing your service development strategy. Companies struggling to build both a strong culture and strong customer relationships must focus on the basics of service maintenance. In our airline example, that means getting customers to their destinations safely, on time, and with their luggage. Companies working from positions of relative strength on the cultural and customer relationship dimensions can move up the hierarchy to improve service performance and innovate. In our chemical company example, an organization with a history of innovation that enjoys close relationships with its customers can innovate to the point of completely transforming itself from a provider of product value to a provider of service value and linked activities. Chapters Three, Four, and Five explore in detail the process of service maintenance, improving service performance, and service innovation.

**Questions for Consideration**

1. What makes the strategy of building a service culture, focusing on a market segment, and linking activities so difficult to implement in your organization? In other words, at which of these processes do you excel, survive, or fall short?
2. What are the defining moments in your organization's saga, and how have they contributed to (or limited) your ability to build a competitive service advantage?
3. What are your organization's stages of service evolution, cultural evolution, and customer relationship evolution? What are the implications for your service development activities?

# Service Maintenance

## Removing Things Gone Wrong

As emphasized in Chapter Two, maintaining a service by removing defects is the foundation of your service development hierarchy whether you are struggling with the basics or aspiring to innovate. The focus of this chapter is service maintenance—removing sources of customer dissatisfaction and exit. This task requires a thorough understanding of the chronology of service production, how to remove things gone wrong, and when to scrap a service process in favor of a completely new one.

Given the frequency with which "things go wrong" in a service setting, it is critically important to view your services from a process perspective.[1] Most defects that occur in a service setting can be traced to a poor service design or process. As a result of these design problems, 70 percent of service defects involve some misunderstanding on the customer's part about how the process is supposed to work.[2] In other words, the potential for service failures is built in from the beginning, often because the company has not taken the time to see how the process looks and works from the customer's perspective. Unfortunately the challenge is inherent in service design. Whereas it's relatively easy to imagine physical goods as they progress through development and production, a service process is more difficult to imagine. Compared to goods, services are more difficult to touch, smell, taste, or try on prior to purchase.

## ■ The Service Maintenance Process

One reason why it is difficult to think of services from a process perspective is that we focus so quickly on the people involved in a service, especially the service providers. Rather than tracing the root cause of a problem back to the design of the service process, companies resort to quick fixes that are poor solutions to a customer service problem. One common quick fix is to just throw more people at the problem. The trouble with relying on quick fixes is comparable to stomping on weeds in your garden or removing only the visible part of the plant. The problem is that the weed keeps growing back.

Let's translate this into a service context that we can all recognize—a baggage claim system. In many airports, the baggage claim system is characterized by a poor queuing of incoming planes to carousels, large crowds (mixtures of passengers, friends, and family), and jumbles of unclaimed luggage. A quick fix is to increase the number of employees patrolling the baggage claim area to help passengers find their luggage and explain how the system works. This "solves" the immediate problem, but the fix is short term. Once the extra employees are reassigned to their regular duties, the weed grows back and the chaos returns. A longer-term solution that begins to address the root of the problem is to improve the signage as a means of helping passengers understand how the system works and where their luggage should be. This may be sufficient if the demands on the system are modest. But the best solution may be to remove the weed completely and plant a flower—that is, to redesign the entire baggage claim system.

Focusing on the basics to improve things gone wrong follows a process well known to those with a quality improvement background. The service maintenance process illustrated in Figure 3.1 is a variation of the quality improvement cycle from total quality management.[3] The process starts with a deliberate decision to challenge the status quo and fix the underlying service system. This decision needs to be explicitly and overtly deployed in your organization if it is to receive sufficient attention

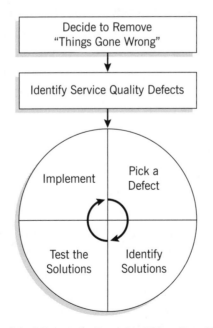

**Figure 3.1.** A Process for Removing "Things Gone Wrong"

for the improvements to be carried out. This is because the success of any solutions that you develop will be highly dependent on your employees' acceptance and implementation. In the rest of this chapter we will work through each subsequent step of the process in Figure 3.1.

## ■ Identifying Defects

After you have chosen to challenge the status quo, your next job is to develop a list of suspects—the defects in your service operation. Identifying things gone wrong is somewhat different from other customer service research. Extensive customer research or participation may not be required to understand what needs fixing. There is usually an awareness of what's going in an organization; employees, management, and customers alike are well aware of the company's basic weaknesses, even if they do not think about them daily. Employees and managers routinely listen to complaints and help solve customer problems. The biggest danger is that they get so used to defending the company's current process that they simply take the problems for granted, allowing them to become a "normal" part of the process. It's a bit like when Sherlock Holmes chides his friend Dr. Watson by telling him, "You look, Watson, but you do not see!"

When problems become so routine that employees are unable even to recognize them as problems, it is best to rely on customers as the primary source of things gone wrong. In some cases, these customer data are already flooding your information systems in the form of frequent complaints. In other cases, customer defect data must come through qualitative research, process mapping, or service audits. For example, Northwest Airlines follows and observes samples of customers as they work their way through airport check-ins, security systems, gates, and baggage claims.[4] As a result, it has identified some correctable problems with signage in the airports that, once fixed, improved customer understanding of the travel process and reduced things gone wrong. In one instance, the signs indicating who should check in where were simply too low for customers to see when crowds formed. Once the signs were elevated, peak customer flows became more orderly and fewer problems were reported. The lesson is that it may not take large sample surveys to locate problems in your service system.

Various relatively simple customer research methods are well suited to identifying things gone wrong and their impact on customers. Many of these methods are what we call transaction specific, in that they focus on customer reactions to specific transactions or service encounters, such as a customer's last trip through an airport or meeting with a financial adviser.

Customer comment cards, such as those at hotels and restaurants, are probably the most common example of a transaction-specific customer feedback tool. Other popular tools and methods for identifying defects in need of improvement are complaint data, focus groups and interviews, more structured interviews such as the critical incident technique and its variants, service process mapping, and service audits. We describe each method in the next sections. In Chapter Four we augment these methods with more comprehensive survey research to understand customer satisfaction and its impact on loyalty and business results.

### Complaint Data

As the focus of service maintenance is on removing sources of dissatisfaction and customer exit, complaint data are both natural and appropriate sources when identifying defects. This assumes, however, that you have an effective customer relationship management (CRM) system or other system for collecting such data. Conceptually, complaint management systems give those customers wishing to remain loyal a chance to do so rather than flee silently to a competitor. But just having a process in place is not enough to gain a representative customer view of things gone wrong. Estimates of dissatisfied customers who choose not to complain run as high as 95 percent.[5]

One major reason that dissatisfied customers choose not to complain is that they view it as not worth the effort. Another reason is that it is unclear or difficult to understand just when, where, and how to complain. Overcoming these barriers requires a process that is easy for customers to understand and use and that encourages complaints at the first point of contact. Customers must also believe that the information will be used to rectify the problem or deliver restitution.[6] Naturally this becomes difficult when the value of the service is small and the complaint process is removed from the experience, as when you lose a coin in a vending machine. Not getting your coffee or candy from the machine may provide the motivation to complain, but the size of the problem and the inconvenience involved in complaining make it unlikely that you will do so. For these reasons, Chuckie Cheese restaurants, which house a number of electronic games for kids of varying ages, have employees deliberately roaming the floor to catch such problems and attend to the game or replenish a customer's tokens. This presence saves customers the effort of having to seek out an employee or store manager. In such cases, having a decentralized and less formal system is far better than relying on a centrally organized complaint system that depends on written statements and forms.

Another factor that can make complaining difficult in a service setting is the intangibility of a service. When a physical good such as an engine won't start, it's clear that there is a problem. In the case of an intangible service, the very existence of a problem can be vague. Was the doctor, lawyer, or waitress being rude or just trying to be funny? Were they ignoring you or giving you time to think? Were they being condescending or trying to be thorough? And the fact that people are involved, people with whom you may have a relationship, makes complaining a sensitive issue.

Before describing other tools and methods for gathering information on defects, let's comment briefly on how complaints should actually be handled. After all, the purpose is more than just to accumulate data for your quality improvement efforts. Even though the complaints coming from your baggage claim area may justify a redesign of the whole system, the complaints still need to be addressed as they occur. The most important rule to remember when addressing customer complaints is that the "punishment should fit the crime." Research shows that the vast majority of customers aren't just looking for a free meal, a check, or airline miles as compensation. Rather, the type or nature of the service failure should dictate what service recovery method is appropriate.[7] Consider a customer who has experienced rude or embarrassing behavior from a service provider. What the customer really needs is an apology. When the service failure does result in an economic rather than social loss, as when time or repair costs are involved, then monetary compensation is appropriate.

### Customer Comment Cards

Customer comment cards are a common source of customer feedback. They are often used to evaluate customer experiences in well-defined episodes or transactions, such as visits to a car dealership or meals at a restaurant. Cards are designed to take a quick pulse and identify problems as they occur. They focus only on the customer's most recent service episode or transaction— their last visit. The response scales are usually very simple so as to encourage customers to fill them out—for example, "Did the service: (1) exceed expectations, (2) meet expectations, or (3) fall short of expectations?"

Customers tend to fill out a comment card when something happens that is out of the ordinary, as when the experience was particularly bad. By definition this leads to a somewhat biased sample of customers. Only those who are very dissatisfied tend to respond, which is a problem common to complaint management systems as well. This limits the value of this information for deciding how to allocate resources. At the same time, they are a way for service managers and front-line service personnel to catch and resolve certain problems in a timely fashion. The interview-based methods described in the next section avoid the problems associated with comment cards and complaint data by proactively including a diverse sample of customers.

### Focus Groups and Personal Interviews

When complaint data and comment cards fail to provide a complete picture of things gone wrong, you should turn to more proactive research. Several qualitative methods can provide a more comprehensive picture of service defects and their impact. Two common qualitative methods are focus groups and personal interviews. For example, one day each year Lufthansa Airlines invites one hundred of its most complaining customers to visit, which is known internally as "horror day." The purpose is to discuss with customers face-to-face the nature of their service problems. During horror day, Lufthansa uses a type of focus group to identify problems and discuss their consequences for customers.

A focus group is a planned, focused discussion involving a small group of similar people. The reason for using groups of similar people is that the similarity makes respondents more willing to open up and freely discuss an issue. A focus group is designed to obtain qualitative data regarding customers' "perceptions, feelings, and manner of thinking about products, services, or opportunities."[8] Typically a moderator leads the discussion, letting participants answer open-ended questions in a group environment. A focus group is essentially a semistructured group interview. Questions flow from the general (for example, "Tell us about your travel experiences over the last twelve months. What have you encountered?") to the specific ("Tell us about your visit to Detroit's new Mid-Field Terminal. Did you notice any particular areas in need of improvement?") as the discussion unfolds. This systematic narrowing in from the general to the specific is what gives focus groups their name. The purpose of moving from the general to various specific topics is to make sure that relevant issues are not missed and that the discussion doesn't sidetrack onto some idiosyncratic point.

Groups vary in size, but they commonly number eight to twelve respondents. When groups get too big, subdiscussions break out, and the moderator may lose control. Sessions are usually recorded, which is useful for later transcription and for educating colleagues.

Just how many focus groups do you need? Remember that the primary purpose of qualitative research, unlike the more systematic satisfaction and loyalty surveys described in Chapter Four, is just to get the relevant issues on the table and explore their consequences. Studies suggest that for a segment of customers, three or four focus groups will capture up to 80 percent of the relevant issues.[9]

One of the main advantages of focus groups is that they are a quick and relatively inexpensive way to gather data. They are particularly well suited to gaining insight into products and services that involve some social interaction. The focus group simulates this social interaction, giving participants an opportunity to trigger and play off of each other's thoughts. Disadvantages are that, in a group situation, participants may feel compelled to respond in a socially acceptable fashion and that some customers are not comfortable talking about certain problems in a group setting.

Personal interviews are a natural alternative to focus groups. In-depth interviews are particularly useful when a deep understanding of particular customers is desired. In Chapter One we saw how SPC used in-depth interviews in the course of its visits to customers' manufacturing facilities to develop a comprehensive understanding of what happens to its products when they reach a customer's site.

The discussion again follows a semistructured interview guide. The misconception surrounding personal or one-on-one interviews is that they are more time and resource intensive than focus groups, in that focus groups allow you to interview more customers in less time. In fact, this tends not to be the case. If there are eight people in a two-hour focus group, each respondent has only fifteen minutes to talk. Once a respondent settles in comfortably with an interviewer, our experience is that personal interviews can provide much more information than what comes out of the "face time" that respondents are given in a focus group. In one study, two one-hour, one-on-one interviews were just as effective at identifying customer needs as a single two-hour focus group, even though there were many more people in the focus group.[10] Not surprisingly, we've seen many companies move away from focus groups to one-on-one interviews as a cost-effective approach to monitoring the voice of the customer. This is particularly true in business-to-business contexts, where customer-supplier relationships may run deep.

**Critical Incident Technique**

A qualitative research method that is particularly well suited to identifying and understanding things gone right and things gone wrong is the critical incident technique (CIT). A critical incident is "a specific example of the service or product that describes either positive or negative performance."[11] The CIT is designed to identify those instances in which customers' expectations are not met, whether in the positive sense of exceeding expectations or in the negative sense of falling short. When you spend an hour trying to get through to a customer service person, or that person hangs up on you, it's something you tend to remember. In this way, the CIT is particularly good at tapping into things gone wrong.

The CIT typically involves an interview in which customers are asked to provide a list of the things that they both like and dislike about the product, service, or company in question. Descriptions of critical incidents should be as specific as possible with respect to particular characteristics of the product or service encountered in the course of the customer's purchase and consumption experience. For example, "I loved it when they went out of their way to drop what they were doing to wait on me" is a classic positive incident; "I hate when you can see employees sitting when there are long lines at the counter" is a classic negative incident. In each case the reference is to a specific behavior or characteristic.

We find it important to augment the generation of critical incidents with subsequent questions to clarify and probe. If the critical incident is too general, ask the customer to be more specific. For each specific incident, probe the customer to elaborate on the significance and consequences of the incident. In Chapter Four we'll use the CIT to identify the potential drivers of customer satisfaction and loyalty that should be included in more formal surveys and used as the basis for performance improvement.

From a service maintenance perspective, these critical incidents serve another purpose. They provide some indication of the relative frequency with which a particular experience goes well versus poorly. Your reliance on these frequencies should depend on the size and representativeness of your sample. The "criticality" of the critical incidents, or their importance to the customer, can also be assessed by asking customers to grade each incident. But perhaps the best insight into the importance of critical incidents is gained by the probing questions, be they regarding the benefit of having something go right or the consequences of having something go wrong.

One limitation of the CIT in a service setting is that customers tend to focus more on service providers than on the service process. They remember that jerk of a teller who ticked them off in the bank rather than the system in which the teller was operating. As noted earlier, it is inherently more difficult to think in terms of things gone wrong with a service process than it is to blame a service provider. A variation on the CIT, called the sequential incident method (SIM), helps address this problem.[12] SIM starts with having the customers trace the service process that they went through. For example, a customer might describe what steps she went through when setting up an investment account online. She might respond, "Well, first I gathered existing account information from my written records and then I found the website. Then I had to create a password, enter the site, and familiarize myself with the options. Then I conducted research to identify an investment and then I made the transaction. Later on I obtained a confirmation by e-mail." After the steps have been made explicit, the interviewer takes the customer back through each step and asks about critical incidents along the way. The SIM thus helps identify things gone wrong with certain steps in a customer service process that might otherwise be ignored.

### Switching Path Analysis Technique

The worst things gone wrong are those that cause a customer to stop doing business with you altogether. Another creative variation on CIT, called the switching path analysis technique (SPAT), is a recent method for understanding why customers switch.[13] SPAT combines elements of CIT and SIM to examine critical incidents that lead to the ending of one relationship and the beginning of another. The switching path is the entire sequence of incidents and service encounters that ultimately lead a customer to switch. As part of SPAT, customers are interviewed six months after switching so as to completely understand not only the switching path but subsequent encounters with the new service provider.

Switching from one company to another is often a longer process than one might think. Just what incident or event actually triggers the switching path may be something external to the relationship, such as a change in the customer's choice set. Triggers also include problems within the relationship, such as poor service or a poorly performing product, and changes in customers' own situations that cause them to reevaluate the relationship. The customer may, for example, move, change jobs, or undergo some change in his or her family. The actual switch occurs when the customer has had a chance to reflect on the critical incident, which may occur quite some time after the event. For example, we employed SPAT analysis to understand those service and product defects that led Volvo automobile owners to switch. We contacted a total of eighty-eight customers who switched from Volvo to another automobile brand, of which twenty-two were willing to tell us their story.

The respondents helped us identify a wide variety of triggers. One respondent's switching path was triggered by a change in his personal situation—a smaller family. When he started looking around at other makes, he realized that they performed better in such areas as fuel consumption, appearance, and noise level. Even though he was happy with the service at the Volvo dealer and had entered the repurchase decision intending to buy another Volvo, these other factors led to the switch. As he said,

*"We are only two in the family nowadays and needed a smaller but spacious car. We chose between V40 and Passat. They were in the same price*

*bracket but I felt that I got more car for the money in the Passat. . . . I got good service at Volvo and that was the real reason for my hesitation to change."*

The following customer comments reveal three other triggers that initiated switching paths. The first relates to the performance of the salespeople.

*"When I bought a new Volvo I was treated like dirt. More than once I made an appointment and took time off from work, and the salesperson was sick and nobody called to cancel the appointment. I had made the trip in vain—poor service. The salespeople have a darn arrogant attitude, almost enough to make you leave. They walk around with an upturned nose and wonder what you are doing there. Young people are overlooked . . . how you are treated has a bearing on how much you trust them. I was disappointed in the treatment and this was the main reason why I changed cars. I will never buy a car from Rejme's again."*

The next one has to do with the vehicle per se.

*"The S40 was not at all what I had in mind. . . . I was not satisfied. It was positively boring, the comfort poor and it was very noisy. I thought both the sales and the service people were good at Rejme's. Unfortunately, I couldn't sell it as fast as I wanted to because I would have lost too much money."*

The last one involves a problem with the personnel in the dealer's service department.

*"It started when we were going to have an alarm system installed and they messed up every time they ordered codes and parts. It should only have taken a few minutes, but I had to make 5–6 trips to get things in order. . . a lot of trouble. I traded cars mostly because of the very poor service. Once I had to have some repainting done on one side. They messed up and again I had to make several trips back. I didn't complain*

*but I felt that they were rather sulky and unpleasant. . . . I believe that they are too big and have lost the feeling for good service."*

Most fascinating is that the triggers that initiate the switching paths so often occur well before the customer is ready to repurchase another automobile. To customers, a triggering event is like a stone in their shoe. If the stone is small, they can live with it, at least for a while. If big, they take it out right away. But once they experience the trigger, the switching path is started. They look at possible alternatives more closely, and when the right offer comes along, they flee. In the second of the four examples, even though the customer bought a Volvo last time around, she was so turned off by the sales process that the switching path for the next purchase had already begun. Companies such as Volvo can use SPAT to understand the relative frequency and importance of incidents related to the car versus the retailer as drivers of customer loyalty. Half of the initial triggers that put our respondents onto switching paths were interactions between customers and employees. In their "moments of truth," employees have a tremendous impact on loyalty, even when most of the customers' consumption involves the day-to-day use of a physical good such as an automobile. When customers are paying so much for a vehicle, they expect a level of service that is comparable to the price. As one of our respondents lamented:

*"They charge 200,000 SEK [about $20,000] for a car, which is your biggest investment after a house. A customer should have some right to expect something. . . . When you are ready to spend so much money and nobody even gets off their ass to meet you—then forget it."*

A car company can do everything right when designing and building a car. Customers can enter the dealership predisposed to buy that car. But because of preventable service defects, they may still switch.

## Service Process Mapping

Our discussion of critical incidents underscores the importance of understanding a service delivery system in detail. There are a variety of mapping tools available for this purpose, which vary in their complexity and focus. Service process maps help service providers visualize the service system as a performance chronology.[14] Figure 3.2 shows a general service process map for a customer's stay at a Ritz-Carlton hotel.

Ritz-Carlton employees operate within a three-stage process that begins with a "warm welcome" when the guest arrives and ends with a "fond farewell" upon his or her departure. In

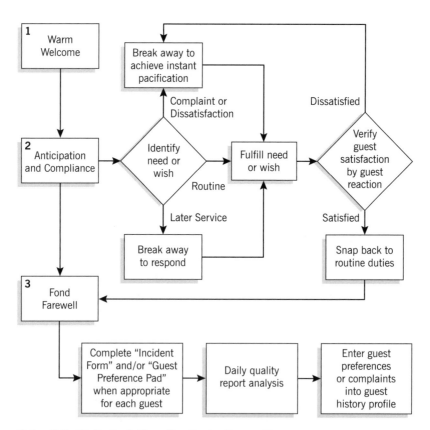

**Figure 3.2.** Ritz-Carlton's Three-Step Service Process Map

between, the "anticipation and compliance" cycle for customer needs is repeated throughout the customer's stay. If a guest expresses a wish or a complaint, there is a subprocess that the employees follow. Whether a housekeeper or manager, the employee confronted with a customer's problem owns that problem through to its resolution. The employee has the flexibility to spend up to $2,000 to correct the problem or handle the complaint. The process may require the employee to "break away" from his or her usual duties to achieve instant pacification or respond with follow-up service. An important part of stage three is to update a guest's database to include how incidents were handled and the guest's preferences. When the guest returns to any Ritz-Carlton hotel, the database is accessed and used to deliver a personalized service experience.

The effectiveness of the process is the stuff of which service legends are made. An automotive executive and friend of ours was recently attending a conference at the Ritz-Carlton in Dearborn, Michigan. When the conference was over and the executive returned to retrieve his sport coat containing his car keys from the coat rack, he realized that another guest had mistakenly taken it home. As our friend lived close to the hotel, his wife was able to drop by with another set of keys. The employee working near the coat check took care of the rest. She followed up with the executive to obtain his coat size and promptly ordered a brand-new coat, reimbursed the cost of the keys, and made sure the coat was delivered to the executive's satisfaction. About two weeks later, the executive's original coat and car keys were delivered back to the hotel by the guest who had taken them by mistake. The employee called the executive and asked if he would like the old coat and keys sent home. On the executive's request, the employee mailed him the keys and gave the coat to charity.

Detailed service maps serve several purposes. They can identify where a service design is overly redundant and may be simplified. They can identify where customers may be taught to make better use of a service. They help companies understand the requisite level of knowledge and skills that employees need to provide a service. Also important, they identify "failure points" where service delivery processes are particularly vulnerable. Figure 3.3 shows a service process map for automobile service that includes eleven specific steps.[15] Step one is Customer Arrival, step two is Repair Order, step three is Post Order, and so on.

This particular type of map uses a cause-and-effect diagram often called a fishbone or Ishikawa diagram after its developer, professor Kaoru Ishikawa.[16] The process illustrated in Figure 3.3 has already been improved over time to eliminate several failure points. For example, "promise time" was added to the sub-process covering preparation of the repair order. Getting the promise time right requires the dealership to have service managers with the requisite knowledge to understand just what is involved and how long it will take to fix. Adding the road test to the process was critical to making sure that the problem was actually solved. And adding the service review stage ensured that customers are charged only for worked performed.

The most complicated of service mapping tools is service blueprinting. Full-blown blueprints include "lines of participation" that communicate those parts of the process that only customers see, that both customers and employees see, and that only employees see. They also include time, cost, and revenue data at each step. Full-blown blueprinting is a time-consuming process, but applicable when accurate cost and revenue estimates are critical.

### Service Audits

Service audits work in conjunction with service process mapping. Once your service process is mapped out, service audits monitor the process. Armed with a detailed checklist of everything that

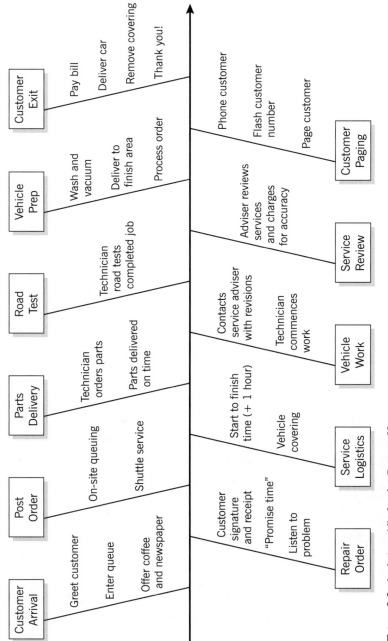

**Figure 3.3. An Automobile Service Process Map**

Customer Arrival
- Greet customer
- Enter queue
- Offer coffee and newspaper

Post Order
- On-site queuing
- Shuttle service

Parts Delivery
- Technician orders parts
- Parts delivered on time

Road Test
- Technician road tests completed job

Vehicle Prep
- Wash and vacuum
- Deliver to finish area
- Process order

Customer Exit
- Pay bill
- Deliver car
- Remove covering
- Thank you!

Repair Order
- Customer signature and receipt
- "Promise time"
- Listen to problem

Service Logistics
- Start to finish time (+ 1 hour)
- Vehicle covering

Vehicle Work
- Contacts service adviser with revisions
- Technician commences work

Service Review
- Adviser reviews services and charges for accuracy

Customer Paging
- Phone customer
- Flash customer number
- Page customer

should occur during the process, service auditors (employees, managers, or customers) move systematically through the process to evaluate the presence or absence of service details. Service audits help companies look at the service process as the customer sees it. Northwest Airlines uses service audits in its airport operations, monitoring sixty-seven details organized into six categories: (1) skycap check-in, (2) lobby/ticket counter, (3) checkpoint security, (4) gate/concourse, (5) luggage claim, and (6) behind the scenes. Within each category, details are further classified into those related to people (Are customer service agents visible, available, smiling, and seeking out customers?), place (Are directional signs posted, accurate, and easy to understand?), or process (Is the queue area orderly?). As described later in this chapter, service audits are a valuable benchmarking tool for obtaining baseline performance metrics and gauging service process improvement.

### ■ Organizing and Prioritizing Defects

Once you have identified defects, your next task is to organize and select which defects to improve. Affinity diagrams and priority setting are useful tools at this stage. The tools are used in a natural progression that starts with an affinity diagram, which is a graphical way to explore problems in order to reach consensus within a group. Figure 3.4 shows a simple hotel example. Affinity diagrams are built by grouping similar service problems into larger groups and subgroups. Studying just what similar problems have in common identifies the root cause. The purpose is not to identify solutions, but rather to understand the underlying nature of service problems. For example, a bed improperly made and dirty cups left in a room can both be categorized under Room Quality and traced back to problems with the room cleaning process. Other problems can be grouped under Staff or Food Service.

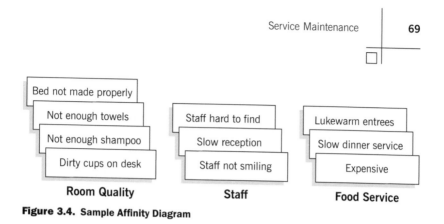

**Figure 3.4.** Sample Affinity Diagram

Having correctly classified problems and identified root causes, you can move on to priority setting. Deciding what to improve requires you to identify the process or processes that have the greatest impact on customers and on which you are performing the poorest. In Chapter Four, when we shift from removing defects (things gone wrong) to improving service performance (things gone right), both impact and performance information will come directly from our analysis of customer data. However, for the moment, prioritizing defects is more of a management decision-making process that takes into account multiple factors or criteria. If prioritizing is done in a group, you might start by voting for the most important defects to improve. If there is disagreement, the votes should be reported to the group and used as the starting point for a discussion to build consensus.

Figure 3.5 shows that the primary criteria to consider when selecting defects are those basic quality factors that "must be there." Being a "must be" factor means that there is little or no trade-off that can compensate for a quality not being present in your service offering. Two basic questions to ask are, Does our performance in this area put customers at risk? and Are we satisfying our customers' basic needs? For example, since September 11, 2001, the primary concern of the airline industry has been to ensure customer safety, hence the overriding emphasis on improving security. Let's face it. Whatever industry you are in, if

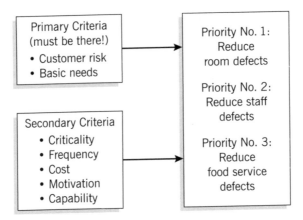

**Figure 3.5. Prioritizing Defects**

you can't provide for basic customer needs and ensure customer safety, you won't stay in business very long.

The lower box in Figure 3.5 shows some secondary criteria that are also important to consider, such as an organization's motivation and ability to make improvements. Beyond the basics, one can't eliminate those defects that, while important to your customers, are impossible for your organization to tackle. Your organization must have the stomach as well as the ability to tackle a particular defect if it is to ensure the level of involvement required to carry through to implementation. Is it possible to find, test, and implement a solution?

Your employees' process knowledge becomes an important input here. It is often the employees with the greatest process knowledge that are able even to see that a problem exists and to identify solutions. This is one reason why employees closest to the process should be part of the prioritizing effort. Another reason is buy-in. The buy-in created at this stage is critically important when identifying benchmarks and metrics for testing proposed solutions and deploying them through your organization.

From an organizational standpoint, don't take on too much at once. Trying to fix a host of problems simultaneously runs the danger of dividing an organization's resources and attention. The exception is full-blown policy deployment, in which multiple quality improvement projects are highly coordinated toward a common objective. Your organization's motivation and ability to make changes must be weighed against such factors as problem frequency (how often a problem occurs), criticality (the severity or number of related problems it might cause), and cost (how expensive it will be to fix).

The right side of Figure 3.5 shows a prioritization of defects for our hotel example. The core or central service that a hotel has to offer is a clean and comfortable room. So if this area is producing as many defects as anywhere else in the operation (or more), it should be the first priority for improvement. Subsequent priorities may depend on trade-offs. For example, removing staff defects may be judged as the second priority to improve if it affects all the customers in the hotel and produces a frequent stream of complaints.

### ■ Identifying Solutions

Once you have prioritized which defects to remove, your next task is to identify solutions. Problem solving is an inherently creative process that starts, at a basic level, with the question, How can we improve? Both customers and employees are important sources of creative problem solving. Indeed, many solutions may already be mentioned in your previously collected complaint data, interviews, critical incident reports, and audits.

Tree diagrams are a valuable tool at this stage of the process. Like affinity diagrams, they assist work groups trying to reach a consensus. They make it easy to identify concrete actions and communicate to others in the organization just why such actions are necessary. Information in a tree diagram flows from the general to the specific. Continuing with our hotel example, Figure 3.6 shows a tree diagram for reducing room defects. Notice that the solutions start at a relatively abstract level before progressing into more concrete solutions and design tasks.

In our simple example, the room defect problems that the hotel guests are experiencing could be resolved using one of two general solutions. The first is to add redundancy. As in our luggage example at the beginning of the chapter, we could just add more staff to an existing service process. Two more specific solutions under adding redundancy are to follow up the room cleaning with an inspection or increase the size of the housekeeping team in order to spot and remove defects. The alternative to adding redundancy would be to redesign the room

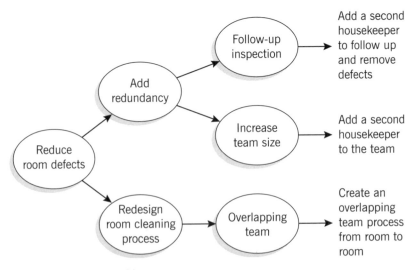

**Figure 3.6. Sample Tree Diagram**

cleaning process in the hopes that one could eliminate the defects more efficiently.

Once the tree diagram is complete and solutions identified, another priority setting occurs among the solutions. Two general considerations apply: (1) the effectiveness of the solution and (2) the ease of implementation. Recall that throwing human resources at the problem may be easier to implement in the short run. In the long run, however, it may be more effective to completely redesign the service process. Later in this chapter we describe how Ritz-Carlton Hotels creatively redesigned their room cleaning process.

### ■ Testing and Implementing Solutions

Your overriding concern when testing and implementing solutions should be quality assurance. This requires that the solution makes sense to the employees and customers involved in the process. Both parties must understand their roles and how the solution ensures a higher level of quality. Physical goods can be quality-tested in a setting removed not only from customers but from most employees as well. In contrast, the co-production that describes service delivery requires that testing directly involve service employees and customers. This is why it's best to test new service processes on a small scale first. The redesigned room cleaning process described later in this chapter was, for example, first tested and implemented at the Ritz-Carlton in Dearborn, Michigan. In other cases, however, complete testing and refinement can occur only on a larger scale, as when there is a single, large service facility involved. For example, it can take months for the service processes in a new airport to function properly. And if you have ever been at a brand-new sports arena on opening day, you might recall just how much of the game you missed waiting for a hot dog or trying to find the bathrooms. No matter how much planning you do, the co-production process will produce surprises.

When implementing a solution it is helpful to have a graphical communication tool. The service process maps described earlier (see Figures 3.2 and 3.3) are good tools for employees to use on a local level to comprehend and apply the solution. Discussing the maps in small groups can facilitate employees' understanding of the improvement and their roles in the process. Holding these discussions tends to be far more productive than communicating roles and responsibilities via memo. Another advantage of using service maps during implementation is that they leave less room for misinterpretation than do more general instructions. Naturally, however, the map should fit the purpose. If the solution involves a more general shift in strategy, then a linked-activities map (such as that for IKEA described in Chapter Two) is the right place to start. If the solution focuses more narrowly on improving a particular service process, then a service process map is appropriate.

Beyond communication, other factors essential in effective implementation are the need to develop appropriate benchmarks and a system of rewards that recognizes improvement. Any process improvement effort requires a clear set of goals and metrics by which the effort will be judged. The service audits described earlier in this chapter are a valuable tool for developing metrics. If the audits are in place prior to implementing a solution, then baselines are already established. This allows you to develop realistic improvement goals. After the implementation, recognizing and rewarding employees who excel at meeting and exceeding the benchmarks go a long way toward improving employee satisfaction and commitment.

In the next section, we describe a case study of process redesign at Ritz-Carlton Hotels. The case illustrates how even a relatively simple process can be completely redesigned to improve service quality.

## Service Process Redesign at the Ritz

Ritz-Carlton Hotels is an Atlanta-based company that manages a chain of luxury hotels. The hotels target industry executives, meeting and corporate travel planners, and affluent travelers. Each hotel pursues the distinction of being the very best in its local market. The Ritz excels on the strength of a comprehensive service quality program for which the company was awarded the Malcolm Baldrige National Quality Award in 1992 and again in 1999. Independent surveys find that 99 percent of Ritz-Carlton guests consider themselves at least satisfied and 80 percent extremely satisfied with their hotel experience.[17]

When Ritz-Carlton won the Malcolm Baldrige National Quality Award for the first time in 1992, it received feedback from the evaluation process on seventy-five areas in need of improvement. Subsequently it used its customer information systems to prioritize a subset of nineteen areas in which to improve. Its goal was to achieve six sigma performance (minimum possible defects) in each area.[18] One of these nineteen areas was room cleaning, a process in which maids worked separately on individual rooms. The first task of the room cleaning improvement team was to map out and completely understand the process, including an extensive use of video recordings to trace the movements of employees in the rooms and measure the time spent on doing various room cleaning tasks. Service audits were used to establish baselines for the number of defects per room.

Once the process improvement team had collected sufficient information, it had to choose between throwing more human resources at the problem or completely redesigning the process. It chose the latter. Figure 3.7 shows the redesigned service process map. The new process uses an overlapping team, where more than one housekeeper is in the room during part of the process, with a team leader. Entering the room first, the team leader prepares the room for cleaning, strips and removes the linens, resupplies the bath, and transports dirty linen and garbage to the cart. Two housekeepers then join the process midstream, one to begin making the bed with the team leader and the other to clean the bathroom. The team leader then services the closet and mini-bar (as needed) before moving on

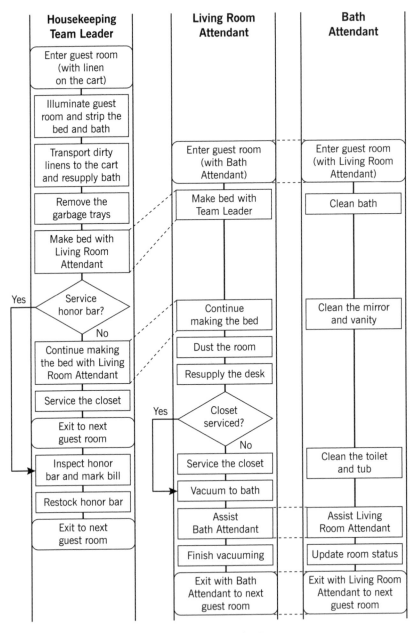

**Figure 3.7. Ritz-Carlton's Redesigned Room Cleaning Process**

to the next room. While the team leader is prepping the next room, the two housekeepers help each other finish cleaning the bath and living rooms.

The result is a more efficient work flow that also increases the number of eyes in each room. The redesigned room cleaning process reduced the average time required per room by 54 percent, from 26.75 minutes to 12.5 minutes, and required no increase in the overall size of the staff. Jobs previously performed separately, such as servicing the honor bar and separating the linens, were now performed by the team. Through the use of blueprints and through careful attention to patterns of movement, the total distance traveled per room by the room cleaning staff was reduced by 64 percent, from 576.25 feet to 209 feet per room, and the number of defects dropped by 42 percent, from 7.4 to 4.3 per room.[19] The redesigned process reflects a healthy dose of common sense. If you've ever made a king-size bed, you can appreciate just how much time and effort is saved by having a helper on the other side. Indeed, it would be easy for a competitor to copy the process; there is no secret formula involved. But this relates back to our model for building a competitive service advantage (described in Chapter Two). The differentiation comes not from any one activity, but rather from a stream of improvements that your culture can support and that are focused on your target customers. The result in this case is a set of linked activities that continue to give Ritz-Carlton a significant competitive service advantage.

## CHAPTER SUMMARY

Whether you are struggling to survive or in pursuit of service excellence, service maintenance is an ongoing process. More often than not, service defects trace back to flaws in the design of the service process. In this chapter, we have laid out a basic process for maintaining service quality. It requires a commitment to removing things gone wrong and a set of tools for identifying service quality defects, setting priorities for improvement, identifying solutions, and testing and implementing those solutions.

Although information on defects is a by-product of complaint management systems, only a subset of customers lodge complaints. For this reason it is important to use proactive research methods to understand your service maintenance problems. The critical incident technique (CIT) has customers explicitly generate things gone wrong and explain their consequences, and the switching path analysis technique (SPAT) looks at those incidents or defects that lead customers to terminate their relationship with the company. Service mapping tools detail the chronology of your service performance to identify defects and failure points in need of fixing.

Once defects have been revealed, you must organize and prioritize them and develop solutions. Affinity diagrams are a convenient way to categorize similar defects and understand their root causes. Prioritizing problems for improvement requires you to consider what qualities "must be" present in a service offering, their frequency and impact on customers, and the company's own ability and motivation to tackle them. Developing solutions is a creative activity that can be made much easier by tapping the knowledge and expertise of your employees and customers, both of whom are engineers in your service production process.

Once you have established an ongoing process for identifying and removing defects, it will be time to move up the service development hierarchy to improve service performance, as reflected by improvements in customer satisfaction, loyalty, and profit. In Chapter Four we'll describe an integrated measurement and management system for doing just that, as our focus shifts from removing things gone wrong to increasing things gone right. This requires an explicit model of how customers perceive your offering, a model we call the lens of the customer. The lens is used to develop a survey measurement and data analysis system that identifies the drivers of customer satisfaction and loyalty from your customers' perspective.

## Questions for Consideration

1. What are the major things gone wrong in your organization that either go undetected or have come to be taken for granted by employees, management, and even customers?
2. What are the root causes of these problems?
3. Given the methods that your organization currently uses, which of the tools and methods described in this chapter (such as the CIT, the SPAT, service process maps, and affinity diagrams) would prove the most valuable to your organization toward understanding and removing things gone wrong?

# Improving Service Performance

## Adding Things Gone Right

S ervice maintenance is an ongoing process of removing things gone wrong and thus not giving customers reasons to leave. Improving service performance is all about adding things gone right and thus giving customers more reasons to stay. In the context of our model of building a strategic service advantage (Figure 2.2), our focus now shifts from fixing existing service activities to linking new activities, developing the next generation of services, and building a competitive service advantage. This process involves more than just spending time talking to customers and following their exploits through your service process. It requires understanding customers' "hot buttons," or just what makes customers very satisfied with and loyal to your company's services. It is also important to understand how customer satisfaction, the relationships you've built, and your company's brand or reputation all drive business performance.

For any substantial business, gaining this understanding requires systematic market studies that detail what underlying benefits you provide customers and how these benefits are created. These studies should look at customers segment by segment and provide the detail required to understand the drivers of customer satisfaction and loyalty by segment. Your attention should also widen beyond current customers to include not only those customers you may have lost but also those you may obtain in the future. The measurement systems developed here in Chapter Four will help you understand sources of competitive advantage and competitor advantage, and identify opportunities to move first.

### ■ An Overall Process for Improving Service Performance

Our process for improving service performance is shown in Figure 4.1. Keep in mind that some aspects of this process, especially the service development cycle described  later in this chapter, apply to both the service improvements described here in Chapter Four and the service innovation process described in Chapter Five.

The first step in the process is to build what we call the lens of the customer. Doing so requires that you view your business from the customers' perspective. The second step is to use the customers' lens as a blueprint for determining the service attributes and benefits that drive customer satisfaction and that help build strong brands and close customer relationships. Customer satisfaction, brand power, and close relationships in turn drive customer loyalty and business performance metrics. The

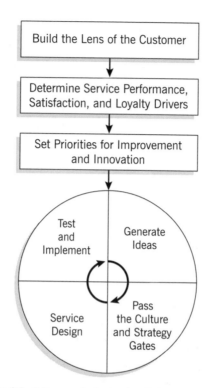

**Figure 4.1.** A Process for Improving Service Performance

more attention paid to building an effective system for measuring and managing satisfaction and loyalty, the better the input for making effective decisions. Indeed, the third step in the process is to set priorities for service quality improvement and innovation.

The most important thing to keep in mind when improving quality and customer satisfaction is that the goal is to optimize rather than maximize. You cannot do everything for every customer—you would never make a profit. But is it possible to determine where you gain the most by improving your service performance? The answer is yes. The key is to build a business model that links your internal quality through to financial performance and then to understand the importance of each link.

A simple example of a service business model is the service-profit chain discussed in Chapter Two. Recall that at Marriott, committed employees take good care of customers, who as a result frequent Marriott hotels and tell their friends and colleagues of their good experiences. That's the Marriott model. The next step would be for Marriott to ask such questions as, Just how much do increases in employee commitment increase customer satisfaction? and Just how much do increases in customer satisfaction increase profits?

In order to reflect on the quality of your current profit model and framework, look at your customer satisfaction questionnaire and ask yourself a few questions: How well does it really measure the quality of your services? Are quality and perceived value being evaluated from your perspective (by department or business process) or according to the benefits that customers desire? Does your survey measure your overall customer satisfaction and resulting brand image or company reputation? Does it measure the strength of your resulting customer relationships and customer loyalty? Finally, do you relate the information in the survey directly to the frequency of purchase, purchase volume, and customer margins? Relating customer satisfaction and loyalty directly to business performance metrics may sound impossible, but it's not. Excellent companies develop explicit, detailed models of how customers view a service offering and the central role that customers play in generating revenues and lowering costs. These companies know where they need to improve in order to get customers to return, buy more, and thus increase the companies' profits.

Once you have clearly identified your improvement priorities, you have the input you need for an ongoing service development cycle.[1] Figure 4.1 depicts this cycle as a process of generating ideas, evaluating those ideas with respect to your service culture and strategy (what we call your culture and strategy gates), developing new service designs, and testing and implementing the new designs. Our experience is that too many firms start this process on the wrong foot by putting too little effort into explicit idea generation. The result is that too many good service ideas elude them until they see them being enacted by a competitor, and thus they spend most of their time emulating competitors' innovations.

There are two aspects of service development that make the process very different from new product development. One is that you must be much more careful in determining whether a new service idea will be able to pass through your company's culture and strategy gates. As emphasized in Chapter Two, your linked activities must be consistent with your target market segments (strategy gate) and service culture (culture gate). Consider X2000, a high-speed train service offered by Swedish State Railways. When the Railways first introduced the X2000 service in 1990, the idea was to make the experience of train travel preferable to air travel. The goal was to enhance the quality and speed of service for businesspeople traveling between major Scandinavian cities, such as Stockholm, Gothenburg, and Oslo. Unfortunately, even though the new trains could travel at a much higher speed than older trains, the service culture was unable to support the level of service required to enhance the overall travel experience. The solution was to form a new company and hire totally new employees to operate the new train service and achieve the needed service levels. Recall from Chapter Two that this is similar to what Continental Airlines did when it found that its culture was incapable of implementing its service strategy. It started from the ground up and built a new culture.

The other aspect that makes new service development so different from new product development is the integral involvement of the customer in the development of service designs and the establishment of prototypes. When a business develops new physical product, the tradition is to translate the voice of the customer into the voice of the designer and engineer.

Although customers may know what kind of performance they want out of an automobile or mobile phone, they are not experts at designing or building it. In contrast, because customers are co-producers in the production and delivery of service offerings (recall the linked activities at IKEA described in Chapter Two), you lose a tremendous source of ideas and creativity if you remove your customers from the design and development process. In Chapter Five we focus specifically on how to innovate by including customers in new service development processes.

In the remainder of this chapter, we describe in more detail the process shown in Figure 4.1. We build on our ongoing case study of IKEA to illustrate how customer satisfaction and loyalty can be modeled and used to set priorities for new service development. The discussion of the first three stages in the process draws on our first contribution to the University of Michigan Business School's Management Series, titled *Improving Customer Satisfaction, Loyalty and Profit: An Integrated Measurement and Management System*. For more details, please refer to that text.[2] The process starts with building the lens of the customer.

### Building the Lens of the Customer

Now you may be saying, "But we already do a good job of gathering customer information and acting on the voice of the customer." The question is whether you really adopt a customer lens or fall into the trap of relying on the lens of the organization. Do you gather information from customers based on how you *think* they view you or based on how they *actually* view you? The lens of the customer views your services and the benefits they provide from your customers' perspective. Looking through this lens, you see yourself as those in the marketplace see you rather than seeing the potentially misleading picture you get from the lens of your organization. Figure 4.2 illustrates the difference in the context of the convenience store industry.

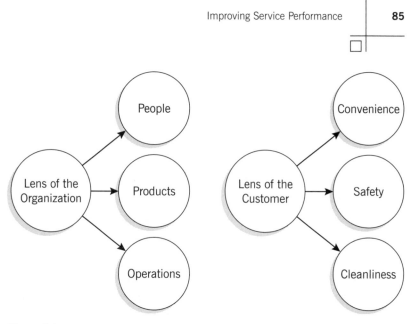

**Figure 4.2.** Whose Lens Is Best?

An executive or owner of a convenience store chain may, for example, view the chain's stores as providing customers with people (service), products (from soft drinks to gasoline), and operations (such as opening hours), each under the management of a different department or business function (see left side of Figure 4.2). The problem is that customers may not share this perspective. Customers view products and services from the standpoint of the benefits they provide and the problems they solve, which may or may not align well with individual business process areas. Convenience store customers look for convenience, safety, and cleanliness (see right side of Figure 4.2). These benefits are not uniquely provided by specific business process areas. Rather, they cut across the people, products, and operating policies of the stores.

Distinguishing between these lenses and adopting the lens of the customer are important for several reasons. Your customers are better at responding to questions from their own perspective. It is your customers' perspective that counts—their perceptions drive their behavior. And understanding customer needs at the customer-benefit level makes it easier to break "out of the box" of your current offerings and come up with new service innovations. Just think about how much easier it is to come up with new and innovative ways to provide convenience and safety as opposed to providing people and products. The latter evoke more concrete images; thinking in terms of them will likely result in relatively small improvements. In contrast, thinking in terms of convenience and safety requires more abstract thinking and can lead to innovative ways to satisfy customer needs. In this way the lens of the customer provides a basis for meeting customer needs that are not currently provided for. For example, innovative convenience store owners provide their customers with convenience by including everything from a variety of hot meal choices to dry cleaning and banking services.

You can use the various qualitative methods discussed in Chapter Three as a basis for developing a lens of the customer, as they all help define and operationalize product and service attributes and the customer benefits they provide. These include one-on-one interviews, group interviews or focus groups, protocol methods (having customers "think out loud" while using or evaluating a product or service), and a variety of observation techniques. However, of all the techniques discussed in Chapter Three, the one that is perhaps best suited to the development of a customer lens is the critical incident technique, or CIT.

The CIT can be used to identify satisfaction drivers for a range of internal and external customers. As described in Chapter Three, it involves using interviews to ask individuals or groups of customers to list and discuss the things they like and dislike about a product, service, or company. Customers are asked to be as specific as possible in describing a single behavior or characteristic of the product or service encountered in the course of the customer's purchase and consumption experience. In our applications of CIT, we augment the generation of critical incidents with subsequent questions that probe and clarify.

If the description of the critical incident is too general, we ask the customer to be more specific. And for each specific incident, we probe the customer for comments on the significance and consequences of the incident. Probing questions will provide you with valuable information for categorizing the incidents into attributes and benefit groupings.

The beauty of the CIT is that it taps into customer perceptions using specific customer memories that are salient and relatively easy for customers to retrieve. Yet these positive and negative incidents are not satisfaction attributes per se. Rather, the incidents reflect some specific level of performance on an attribute where customers' experiences vary. An attribute, in this context, describes the more concrete aspects of the product or service (such as size, speed, price, and so on). Consider an example in which a convenience store customer comments positively on the abundance of parking spaces at her local convenience store and how fast the checkout people are. A different customer may, in contrast, comment negatively on the scarcity of parking spaces at his store and how slow the checkout people are. The researcher's job is to identify that both customers are referring to the same two concrete attributes on which they receive very different levels of performance, the availability of parking and the speed and efficiency of the checkout person.

Once the critical incidents are coded into attributes, the attributes are then coded or sorted into a set of benefit categories. In this sorting process, the researcher relies on his or her judgment (as to what the customer is referring to) and on information obtained in the probing questions. An example of attribute sorting is shown in Table 4.1. The goal is to sort them into benefits that describe the more general or abstract qualities that customers derive from the attributes. You may notice that this process is similar to using the affinity diagrams described in Chapter Three to group quality attributes into higher-level categories. You may ask customers themselves to perform the sorting process if the groupings are unclear.

**Table 4.1.** Benefit Categories and Attributes for Convenience Stores

| Benefit Categories | Attributes |
| --- | --- |
| Service | Accuracy of the checkout |
| | Friendliness of the employees |
| | Attentiveness of the employees |
| | Grooming and appearance of the employees |
| Products | Stock or availability of products |
| | Brand names of products |
| | Variety and selection of products |
| | Freshness of the coffee |
| | Freshness of products |
| Store layout | Ability to find what you need |
| | Neatness and orderliness of displays |
| | Feeling or sense of fun you get when walking through the store |
| Prices | Overall value |
| | Competitiveness of store prices |
| | Competitiveness of gasoline prices |
| | Frequency of sale items |
| Cleanliness | Cleanliness inside the store |
| | Cleanliness of the bathrooms |
| | Cleanliness outside the store |
| Convenience | Convenience of the location |
| | Hours of operation |
| | Speed and efficiency of employees |
| | Availability of parking |
| Safety | Lighting of the premises |
| | Ability to see what is happening in the store |
| | Feeling of safety and security |
| Motorist services | Accuracy of signs, gauges, and meters |
| | Ability to pay at the pump |
| | Availability of car wash |
| | Availability of air and water for vehicles |
| | Working operation of the equipment |
| Separate takeout | Variety and selection of takeout food |
| | Accuracy of food preparation |
| | Quality of takeout food |

### Modeling Service Performance, Satisfaction, and Loyalty Drivers

The CIT process yields the customer lens that is the basis for both developing surveys and subsequently analyzing the data. Ultimately, the attributes and benefit categories that make up the lens become the drivers of customer satisfaction in a quantitative customer satisfaction and loyalty model. Figure 4.3 illustrates a sample conceptual model that incorporates the lens of the convenience store customer derived from Table 4.1.

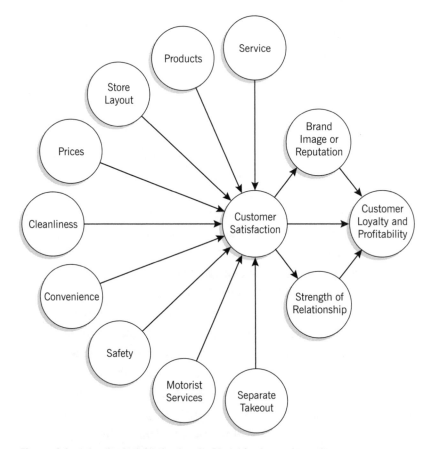

**Figure 4.3.** A Quality-Satisfaction-Loyalty Model for Convenience Stores

A recent and interesting evolution in satisfaction models is reflected in Figure 4.3. Notice that it incorporates two summary evaluations in addition to customer satisfaction as drivers of customer loyalty and profitability. The direct effect of satisfaction on loyalty captures the degree to which customers' purchase and consumption experiences directly impact loyalty. Using brand image or company reputation measures as another means of explaining loyalty captures customers' attitudes about the brand per se, such as the degree to which the brand fits a customer's personality or the "buzz" on the street, and the direct effect this has on customer loyalty and profits. For a convenience store, the measures here might include the reputation of the chain and the reputation of the local store that a customer typically visits.

Adding strength of relationship to the model captures those factors that create "stickiness" in the relationship. Even when customers have a poor attitude about the brand and satisfaction is low, these are the factors that cause the relationship to survive or even grow. Survey measures here might include the customer's commitment to maintaining a relationship with a particular convenience store chain, the economic costs incurred if the customer is forced to use another chain, or the quality of the chain's loyalty or frequent customer program. Naturally, how customers evaluate their experiences (customer satisfaction) has a direct effect on both their evaluations of brand image or reputation and the strength of relationship.

Some satisfaction and loyalty models also contain an overall evaluation of perceived value, or what customers get for what they pay. This is especially common in business-to-business models where purchasing agents are constantly monitoring a vendor. It can also be the case in business-to-consumer models where purchase patterns and relationships are just evolving. When perceived value is included, we like to model at least product and price as having direct effects on perceived value, and perceived value as having a direct effect on both satisfaction and loyalty. However, in most mature businesses, consumers or customers are not monitoring perceived value per se. In the convenience store model, for example, perceived value is just another attribute of a store's prices that, along with all of the non-price-based benefits, drive customer satisfaction.

Because improving service quality and satisfaction is the best way to build reputation, relationships, and loyalty, we focus here on how to improve your customers' service experience. We do not describe in detail how to develop surveys using a satisfaction and loyalty model, how to collect data, or how to analyze that data. As mentioned earlier, detailed processes for these tasks are available in our book *Improving Customer Satisfaction, Loyalty, and Profit*. But it is important to understand generally how information is extracted from customer survey data to illuminate competitive strengths, weaknesses, and opportunities.

*Quantifying the Model*
Priority setting, which we cover in detail later in the chapter, must take into account both how your firm performs on the various benefits and attributes in the model *and* how much impact the benefits and attributes have on satisfaction and subsequent loyalty. Generally you want to improve on those drivers of satisfaction that are important to customers and on which you currently fail to perform. Referring back to Chapter Two and Figure 2.1, these are areas in which competitors are likely to have an advantage. Many satisfaction measurement systems in the service industry continue to rely on the "gap" model to obtain performance and importance information. According to the gap approach, priorities are identified by calculating the difference between customers' direct ratings of attribute importance (or desired performance) and direct ratings of actual performance (in other words, importance minus performance).[3] The primary advantage of direct importance scale ratings and the gap model is

their ease of implementation. They require minimal analysis (plotting averages and calculating difference scores) and can be easily understood at various levels in an organization, from front-line service personnel to CEOs.

Yet there are several problems associated with using direct importance ratings. There are rarely significant differences in importance ratings among the top-rated fifteen to twenty attributes in a survey. As a result, the importance scores don't provide much information—most of the variance in the "gaps" is driven by differences in perceived performance from attribute to attribute. Research also shows that the importance measures or weights that people report and those that they use when making a decision often differ dramatically. Foremost, direct importance ratings don't take into account the impact that changes in quality are likely to have on customers.

Our research has found that it is more objective and diagnostic to statistically derive importance as the impact that various attributes and benefits have on satisfaction. Customers indicate how they perceive a product or service to perform on a number of attributes as well as their overall satisfaction and loyalty. Variation in performance and satisfaction across different customers' ratings allows you to estimate (using regression or regression-based statistical techniques) the impact (beta coefficient) that different aspects of quality and value have on satisfaction and loyalty. Because it is more objective, statistically determined importance can avoid many of the problems that one can encounter when using direct importance ratings.

But keep in mind that even the quality of statistical estimates can vary significantly. The key question is whether or not the estimation uses the lens of the customer. The lens of the customer, which is derived from a thorough analysis of qualitative research, tells us just which attributes go together in the customer's mind. By combining multiple attribute ratings together into benefit indexes, the lens provides a means of reducing co-linearity among the satisfaction drivers; it increases their statistical independence. The result is a set of benefit and attribute importance weights that are superior to those that can be collected directly from customers.

We recommend using a nontraditional type of principal-components regression (PCR) to leverage your lens of the customer. Traditional PCR performs a factor analysis of all the attribute ratings simultaneously to produce a set of independent components or, in this case, product and service benefits that are analogous to the lens of the customer as we have described it. The weakness of this traditional approach is that it is too data driven; the factor analysis blindly dictates a "lens" of its own. It makes no use of the benefit clusters that we developed into the lens of the customer by using the insights of qualitative research. In contrast, the approach we recommend uses the benefit groupings or clusters in the lens as a theory or model to structure the PCR analysis. Again, for details on how to derive attribute and benefit impact and performance scores from a satisfaction survey, please refer to our earlier book.

*An Example from the Convenience Store Industry*
We will use results from a survey by the National Association of Convenience Stores and the benefit information in Table 4.1 to illustrate a PCR analysis.[4] The data include survey interviews from a national (U.S.-based) sample of convenience store customers. A computer-aided telephone interview was used to collect the data. Performance in each of the benefit areas is a weighted average of how customers rate the convenience store on the attributes that make up the benefit. Customers rated the attributes using a scale from 1 (poor performance) to 10 (excellent performance). Impact, our measure of importance, is the degree to which an improvement in each benefit results in an increase in

customer satisfaction. For example, an impact of 0.27 for a bene-fit such as safety (see Figure 4.4) means that a 10 percent increase in perceived safety results in a 2.7 percent increase in overall satisfaction.

Figures 4.4 and 4.5 show benefit-level impact-versus-performance charts for two different types of convenience stores, 7-Eleven (an international franchised chain) and "mom-

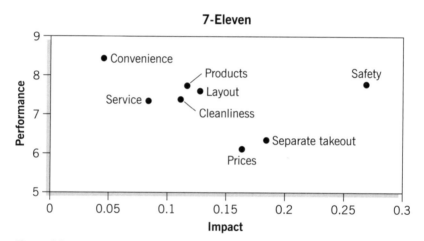

**Figure 4.4.** Benefit-Level Impact-Versus-Performance Chart for 7-Eleven Stores

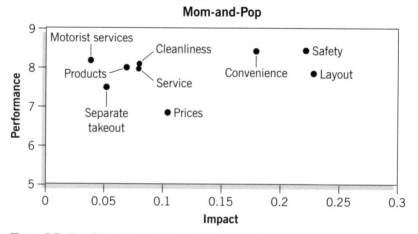

**Figure 4.5.** Benefit-Level Impact-Versus-Performance Chart for Mom-and-Pop Stores

and-pop" stores that are neither franchised nor part of a chain. There were 154 customers in the 7-Eleven sample and 257 customers in the mom-and-pop sample. (Similar analyses that are not shown here provide impact-versus-performance scores for each set of attributes within a benefit area.) Recall that the most essential areas to improve are those where impact is high and performance is weak. In other words, we want to ask, In what areas that are important to customers are we falling short and, hence, competitively vulnerable?

The results for 7-Eleven show separate takeout and prices as both having relatively high impact and low performance, making them good candidates for improvement. For the mom-and-pop stores there are not the same glaring weaknesses. The lower impact of separate takeout is likely because customers don't look for mom-and-pop stores to be integrated with large food store chains such as Subway or Pizza Hut. The lower impact of prices for these stores is likely due to the high impact and strong performance, or competitive advantage, that these stores have in three other areas (convenience, safety, and, to some degree, store layout) compared to only one high-impact, strong performance area for 7-Eleven (safety).

Given the data in the two graphs, it is not surprising that customer satisfaction (measured on a 10-point dissatisfaction to satisfaction index) is significantly higher for the mom-and-pops (7.8) than it is for the 7-Elevens (7.1). The results illustrate how the better a service provider performs in areas of high importance to its customers, especially non-price-related areas, the better its overall value proposition and the lower the impact of prices on satisfaction. The results for prices further illustrate the need to benchmark on the competition. Whereas prices might be a potential weakness for the mom-and-pop stores when judged in isolation, benchmarking against 7-Eleven shows how the latter performs lower on the attractiveness of its prices, and these prices have a higher impact. That is, they create more dissatisfaction.

**Setting Priorities for Improvement and Innovation**

Metrics such as those in Figures 4.4 and 4.5 can help you make fact-based decisions, but they don't make the decisions for you! As our discussion of the convenience store impact-versus-performance charts suggests, deciding which service performance areas to improve requires a careful consideration of your situation, your competitors' situations, the costs involved, and, most important, your strategy. Improving on those attributes that currently define your service benefits is continuous improvement; creating new ways to deliver on those benefits is innovation. The important point here is that people make decisions, whether it is the convenience store executive who sets corporate priorities, the front-line service manager who translates these priorities into policies and procedures, or the service worker who translates policies and procedures into concrete actions.

Your priorities must take into account the business context, including the customer or market segment involved. Whereas business travelers look to a hotel for a good night's sleep, vacation travelers place more value on the hotel's amenities and staff. A careful consideration of the market context allows you to anticipate how improvements in one service area may affect other areas. Consider the case of a ski resort that recently introduced a package of cable TV movies and features as an add-on to their basic room rates. Although the guests gave the resort high marks for the added feature, it caused the guests to spend less time skiing, shopping, and eating in the restaurants. In the end, the resort lost money on the improvement.

A simple marketing framework that helps managers think strategically about which areas to improve is the strategic satisfaction matrix shown in Figure 4.6.[5] The matrix helps classify the benefits and attributes of a service offering according to their strategic importance, in a manner similar to the Venn diagram used in Chapter Two (Figure 2.1). Just what constitutes high or

| Low Impact and Strong Performance Maintain or reduce investment or alter target market | High Impact and Strong Performance Area of competitive advantage—maintain or improve performance |
|---|---|
| Low Impact and Weak Performance Inconsequential—do not waste resources | High Impact and Weak Performance Area of competitive vulnerability—focus improvements here |

**Figure 4.6.** Strategic Satisfaction Matrix

low impact or performance is, of course, a function of both the absolute levels (for example, a performance of 9 on a 10-point scale) and competitive benchmarks (for example, a performance that is 1 point higher than your closest competitor on a 10-point scale).

According to the matrix, the most cost-effective areas to improve are those that are both important to customers and on which your company is performing poorly. Changes in these areas focus resources and quality improvements where they have the greatest impact on satisfaction and subsequent loyalty and profitability. These are your competitive vulnerabilities. If these needs are better met by a competitor, the customer's business is lost (see Competitor Advantage area in Figure 2.1). Activities in which performance and impact are both high represent your firm's competitive advantage (see Competitive Advantage area in Figure 2.1). It is essential to maintain your performance on these drivers. If the goal is to deepen your competitive advantage in an area, continue to improve or innovate around it. In our convenience store example, consider the three areas in which the mom-and-pop stores have high impact and strong performance. Because they have no glaring high impact–weak performance areas, they may choose to continuously improve on one of their strengths, such as store layout.

Clearly, where impact is low and performance is weak, customers are telling you not to waste resources improving. More interesting is the low impact–strong performance cell of the matrix. This may be an area where resources have been wasted in the past because the benefits and attributes are not important to customers. These are areas from which you should reallocate resources to activities that are more important to customers (as shown in Figure 2.1). Recall that some benefits in these areas should be watched, in case they become important to customers in the future. Consider "environmental friendliness," for example, which was not regarded as important by many customers until recently. Companies that predicted the importance of this area and prepared their business accordingly clearly gained an advantage.

The low impact–strong performance cell may contain drivers of satisfaction that customers consider to be basics as we defined the term in Figure 2.1. In other words, it may include benefits and attributes that are consistently provided to customers (such as friendly service personnel) by all relevant competitors. Although they are important in an absolute sense, they have little to no impact on satisfaction because there is little differentiation in their performance. The danger is that a reduction in performance quality would increase their impact on satisfaction, a danger often referred to as a slippery slope. For example, it is interesting to observe how convenience is a basic from 7-Eleven's perspective but not for the mom-and-pops. This is because 7-Elevens tend to be located in areas with other convenience stores, making them equally convenient, whereas mom-and-pop stores are in small market or urban locations where convenience remains a competitive advantage.

### New Service Development Cycle

The output of priority setting is a set of abstract service benefits and more concrete service attributes that are in need of improvement. Following our overall process for improving service performance (illustrated in Figure 4.1), these priorities become input to a new service development cycle. This part of the process has four steps: idea generation, passage through the strategy and culture gates, service design, and testing and implementation.

*Idea Generation*

New service ideas should be explicitly generated from a variety of sources. Too many service organizations believe that it is rather easy to generate ideas, thus dismissing the need for a formal process for doing so.[6] Successful service organizations establish explicit systems and procedures to generate ideas on an ongoing basis.

One important source of new ideas is, of course, competitors or admired peers. In some idiosyncratic service industries such as banking, competitors are often the main source of new service ideas.[7] The problem, of course, is that it is difficult to do much more than catch up to competitors, as this type of service development is reactive and defensive. And customers often remember who the true innovators really are. As emphasized earlier in the chapter, another important source of new service ideas is customers themselves. The more innovative you want to be, the more important it becomes to elicit ideas directly from customers. As co-producers in the service process, they will come up with ideas that competitors don't yet have. Involving customers directly in the new service development process is the focus of Chapter Five.

Employees have long been considered an important source of new service ideas. Spanning the boundary between your company and its customers, your service employees gain extensive process knowledge and face-to-face service experience that makes them a valuable source of ideas. Yet their potential is often wasted, partly because many companies lack a formal process for capturing and disseminating employees' ideas. Brainstorming tools such as the affinity diagrams described in Chapter Three are simple ways to begin formalizing the generation and dissemination of your employees' ideas.

*Passage Through the Strategy and Culture Gates*

As a second step in the service development cycle, it is critical that a service organization evaluate its ideas by asking two key questions. First, is the idea in line with its business strategy or focus? Second, has the company established an effective service culture to support the idea? These questions directly reflect the model for building a competitive service advantage, discussed in Chapter Two. Competitive service advantages are defined by the unique set of linked activities that you provide (recall the linked-activities map for IKEA, shown in Figure 2.4). The complex and often delicate nature of an entire set of linked activities requires that you remain focused on a given set of customers and have a culture in place that supports the activities (recall the X2000 railway service).

It follows that the addition of any new service or activity must be consistent with your strategy and values. The essence of strategy is choosing what *not* to do,[8] as when IKEA refuses to sell furniture that is too expensive or too complicated to build. Similarly, as IKEA's focus is on serving the many in the middle and selling furniture at prices these customers can afford, it would be inconsistent with IKEA's culture and strategy to form an elitist club of select customers. Instead IKEA has a Family Club that is open to everyone, from suppliers and employees to customers. The idea is to maintain a family that works together, which is a core value of IKEA's founder, Ingvar Kamprad.

Figure 4.7 is our adaptation of what Berry calls strategy connections. It shows how service execution and linked activities should relate to your core strategy and values.[9] In Chapter Two we described Berry's seven commonly held values that sustain excellent service organizations: innovation, excellence, joy, teamwork, respect, integrity and social profit (see Table 2.1), and we showed how many of these values pervade IKEA's strategy. This emphasis on core values recognizes that a service company is more a community of human beings than a collection of

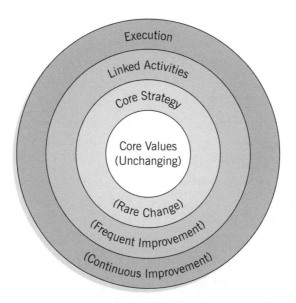

**Figure 4.7.** Our Adaptation of Berry's "Strategy Connections"

equipment, labor, and capital. Your own community holds the core values and beliefs that must support any new service improvements or innovations. Your community must also understand how your values and norms form a cogent business model (such as the employee-customer-profit chain). This underscores the importance of communicating the logic of any new service or activity and its consistency with your values and overall service strategy.

A successful service strategy, according to Berry, focuses on: (1) serving a specific market need rather than on marketing a specific product for that need, (2) underserved market needs, (3) serving chosen markets in a superior manner, and (4) focusing only on the core strategy.[10] Berry's concept of strategy connections conveys the importance of the strategy and culture gates. It is also completely consistent with our guiding process for creating a competitive service advantage: build your culture, stay focused, and link activities!

## New Service Design

The third step in the service development cycle is to design the new service. Before fleshing out and testing the details of the design, you must consider the new service concept in a holistic way. According to Edvardsson's "service logic," this service concept must capture (1) the desired customer outcome, (2) the prerequisites needed to achieve the outcome, and (3) the customer process.[11]

You supply the prerequisites for a service in the form of an infrastructure, human resources, and organizational resources. The quality of the eventual customer outcome (the benefits or problem resolution that customers desire) is dependent on the quality of the prerequisites. In our IKEA example from Chapter Two, the linked activities surrounding modular furniture design and low-cost manufacturing (those linked activities in the bottom half of Figure 2.4) are essential prerequisites for IKEA's service concept. In the customer process, customers actively or passively participate by carrying out different activities. For IKEA these include the linked activities related to self-service and self-selection (see the top half of Figure 2.4). The customer outcome, of course, is the outcome of the linked activities: to provide the best possible value in furniture and home products for the many in the middle.

Edvardsson's point is that what service companies really offer their customers is not a service per se but service opportunities—that is, the opportunity to make use of the company's prerequisites. For the service to be effective, customers must clearly understand and be able to apply service prerequisites, from the service company's available technical resources to its administrative routines and procedures. The design of an effective Internet banking service, for example, must provide customers with the technology necessary to access their accounts and with easy-to-follow processes for paying bills, transferring money, and making financial investments. This service logic applies to physical products in a service setting as well. A washing machine, after all, is simply a prerequisite for clean clothes.

The service logic provides a first delineation in the service design process. What prerequisites will you need, and what customer processes must be linked to these prerequisites? How do your prerequisites help clarify the customer's role in the process? Finally, how do both your prerequisites and the customer come together to deliver a customer outcome? The easier these processes are for employees and customers to learn and participate in, the higher the quality, satisfaction, and loyalty that results.

The next step is to develop in more detail just how the new service idea or linked activity will actually work. For example, just how much will the customer interact with the staff, with other customers, and with physical and technical resources? This often requires breaking the service down into a number of smaller processes using the service mapping and blueprinting tools described in Chapter Three. As described next, fleshing out the specifics of the new service design is an integral part of the testing and implementation phase of service development.

### Testing and Implementation

The testing and implementation of new service activities have two overriding goals. The first is to ensure that a new service interacts with and affects other linked activities in your overall service concept as planned. The second is to ensure that both customers and employees in the system learn and behave as planned. Tax and Stuart have developed a useful planning cycle for the successful integration of new services, as illustrated in Figure 4.8.[12]

Step one is to audit your current service system, which includes an evaluation of the customers' role in the service system; the present processes used to deliver the service; the benefits provided to customers; the skills, capabilities, and personality traits of the participants; and the physical facilities. Step two is

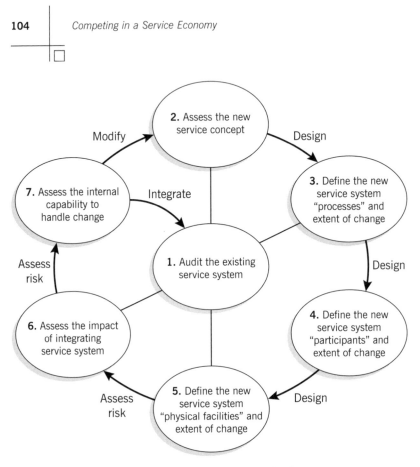

**Figure 4.8.** Tax and Stuart's Planning Cycle for New Service Systems

to assess the new service concept from a market perspective. For example, what combinations of features is the market actually looking for? What prices should be charged? Is the offering going to appeal primarily to new or existing customers?

Steps three, four, and five involve assessing the new service design from the perspective of processes, participants, and physical facilities. A good example of steps three and four is the redesigned housekeeping process for Ritz-Carlton described near the end of Chapter Three (see Figure 3.7). The extent of change in that process is that a team of employees now enters and leaves a room at different times. Step four includes the preparation of job descriptions, selection criteria, appraisal systems, training programs, and compensation schemes. For the Ritz, step four addresses how multiple employees now work together to make the housekeeping process more efficient and error free. An output of the service development process is often a proposed or redesigned physical facility. Step five in Tax and Stuart's planning cycle defines and evaluates the extent of change in the facility.

A good example related to step five is Best Buy's Concept V store layout, shown in Figure 4.9.[13] Best Buy has a reputation as an innovative and creative retailer of home electronics, appliances, and related products. Previous store layout concepts rated highly on the clarity of sight lines and on communication of selection and value. Yet 60 percent of Best Buy sales came from 20 percent of the floor space. The recently introduced Concept V stores incorporate several design improvements to address this problem. A central loop has been introduced, so that customers entering the store can immediately see the latest digital and entertainment products. The clear and wide central walkways are designed to disperse traffic throughout the store. Moving the music section, which accounts for 55 percent of Best Buy's business, to the left side of the store is also designed to improve traffic patterns.

The overall purpose of steps three, four, and five is to clarify service system requirements and resolve conflicts. Implementing a new store concept often occurs on a small scale at first (as in a subset of stores or a particular geographical area) before finalizing any changes and implementing them systemwide. For example, Best Buy has been testing and evaluating its Concept V stores in new locations before it allocates the resources to redesign existing stores.

In step six of the planning cycle, the goal is to assess the impact of integrating the new service system with the original system. A particularly useful planning technique at this step is quality function deployment (QFD). Originally developed for

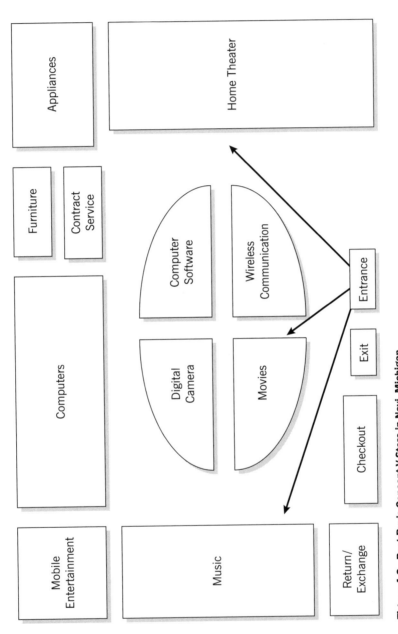

**Figure 4.9. Best Buy's Concept V Store in Novi, Michigan**

manufactured goods and recently adapted to service settings, this tool is a systematic process for translating the service design into concrete operating procedures and contingency plans in an organization.[14] QFD is an inherently cross-functional tool that, when applied in a service context, involves decision makers from human resources, service operations, and marketing. We describe QFD in more detail in the next section.

The seventh and final step in the cycle is to assess the capability of the firm to implement and manage the change. Your organization needs to evaluate its existing capabilities to ensure that they match the specifications of the combined service systems. Now that the service is more concretely designed and linked to existing activities, does it still pass the strategy and culture gates? If the assessment is that your organization is not up to handling the change, three alternative courses of action are available: (1) revise your objectives, (2) choose to provide the new ideal service but in a different location, or (3) move ahead with the new service knowing that the quality of your service offering as a whole may be compromised. Once the planning cycle is completed, the service development cycle moves to the implementation phase, which includes marketing and launch. At this point the process of monitoring and maintaining service quality begins.

*Quality Function Deployment*
Quality function deployment (QFD) is a useful tool for designing and implementing a new service. Its primary purpose is to help you focus on what qualities are most important to your customers and ensure that those qualities exist in the ultimate product or service. The QFD application is usually documented in a series of matrixes. Originally developed in a manufacturing context, QFD translates the voice of the customer into the voice of the engineer before translating it further into parts, designs, and

manufacturing. The core principle of QFD is a systematic transformation of subjective customer requirements and expectations into increasingly objective and measurable product, service, and process parameters. This core principle of using customer information to drive changes in your service offerings and organization has been our focus throughout Chapter Four.

Using QFD for our purposes requires adapting the tool to apply more in a service context.[15] Because services are coproduced between customers and employees or service systems, it is often impossible to distinguish between key parts characteristics and key process operations. As a result, service applications of QFD usually focus on translating customer requirements (the convenience of a hotel) into key service qualities (transportation to and from the airport), service functions or activities (a shuttle service), and eventually into service process designs (shuttle scheduling and contingency plans).

### Satisfaction Modeling and Priority Setting at IKEA

In this last section of the chapter, we continue our case study of IKEA to illustrate how the customer satisfaction and loyalty modeling described earlier in the chapter provides input to a service QFD application.[16] The research looks at customer satisfaction with and loyalty to an IKEA store in the United States.[17] Figure 4.10 shows a subset of the attributes and benefits that make up the lens of the IKEA customer as derived from a series of critical incident interviews. The benefits included here are the store layout, the in-store experience, perceived value, and ease of assembly of the furniture. Each benefit is a combination of a number of more concrete attributes. The in-store experience is, for example, a combination of the ability to browse, the variety of styles and colors, the uniqueness of the shopping experience, and the experience's being more an adventure than a hassle. The four benefit areas drive customer satisfaction (measured using three overall evaluations of the customer experience), which in turn drives customer loyalty (measured using likelihood of repurchase and recommending to a friend).

Figure 4.10 includes the estimated statistical impacts of each benefit area on satisfaction and of satisfaction on loyalty. Also included are the levels of performance, rated on a 10-point scale, for each benefit and for satisfaction and loyalty. Recall from our earlier discussion that these performance levels are indexes or weighted averages of responses to the survey items shown in the boxes.

The customer's in-store experience has the greatest impact on satisfaction (0.42), and IKEA performs well on this benefit (8.40). As this is a competitive advantage for IKEA, it should be continuously improved. In order to drive changes in the overall service and product offering, this impact and performance information becomes input to the first matrix of QFD. Figure 4.11 presents a partial QFD matrix for our IKEA example, focusing on the in-store experience. Customer needs constitute the rows in the matrix; different store functions or areas constitute the central columns.

The columns labeled 1 through 5 contain the satisfaction modeling information required to set priorities among the attributes. Column 1 contains a measure of the impact that each attribute has on its benefit area. By multiplying these impacts by the impact that each benefit has on satisfaction (column 2) we obtain the estimated QFD importance of each attribute (column 3). It is often helpful to interpret these measures as percentages across the attributes of a benefit, which are provided in column 4. Finally, column 5 presents performance benchmarks by benefit and attribute (on the 10-point poor-to-excellent performance scale). (Not shown here, but typically included in QFD applications, are competitive benchmarks for assessing whether performance is relatively strong or weak.) In this example, *variety of styles and colors* has the greatest impact on in-store experience (0.24) and moderately strong performance (8.3); *more an adventure than a hassle* has the second highest impact (0.17) and strong performance (8.8). As competitive advantages that are central to IKEA's linked activities, both attributes are candidates for improvement.

The next step is to determine which service quality areas have the greatest effect on these attributes and targeting them for improvement. The matrix contains just a sample of weights that capture the effect that

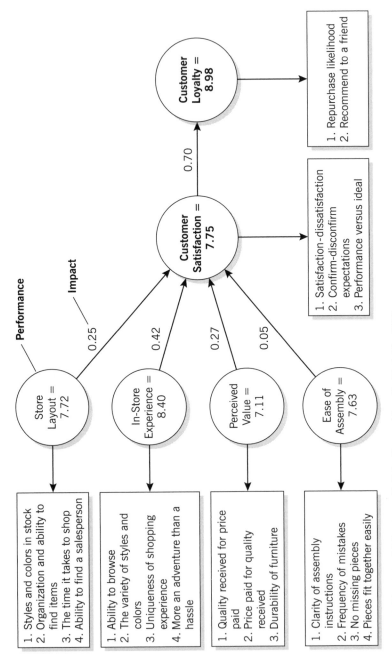

**Performance**

**Impact**

Store Layout = 7.72

1. Styles and colors in stock
2. Organization and ability to find items
3. The time it takes to shop
4. Ability to find a salesperson

In-Store Experience = 8.40

1. Ability to browse
2. The variety of styles and colors
3. Uniqueness of shopping experience
4. More an adventure than a hassle

Perceived Value = 7.11

1. Quality received for price paid
2. Price paid for quality received
3. Durability of furniture

Ease of Assembly = 7.63

1. Clarity of assembly instructions
2. Frequency of mistakes
3. No missing pieces
4. Pieces fit together easily

0.25

0.42

0.27

0.05

Customer Satisfaction = 7.75

1. Satisfaction-dissatisfaction
2. Confirm-disconfirm expectations
3. Performance versus ideal

0.70

Customer Loyalty = 8.98

1. Repurchase likelihood
2. Recommend to a friend

**Figure 4.10. A Partial Customer Satisfaction and Loyalty Model for IKEA**

++ Strong positive relationship
\+ Positive relationship
– Negative relationhip

| | | 1 | Quality of paths, showrooms, and exhibits | | Quality of customer involvement | | . . . | | 2 | 3 | 4 | 5 |
|---|---|---|---|---|---|---|---|---|---|---|---|---|
| | | Attribute impact on benefit | Number of routes through store | Number of exhibits | Quality of preparation (before) | Quality of preparedness (during) | | | Benefit impact on satisfaction | Estimated importance (1) x (2) | Absolute importance (3)/sum(3) | Performance |
| Layout | . . . | | | | | | | | | | | |
| In-store experience | Ability to browse | 0.09 | ++ | + | | | | | 0.42 | 0.038 | 14% | 8.2 |
| | Variety of styles and colors | 0.24 | | ++ | | | | | 0.42 | 0.101 | 36% | 8.3 |
| | Uniqueness of shopping experience | 0.16 | + | + | + | + | | | 0.42 | 0.067 | 24% | 8.1 |
| | More an adventure than a hassle | 0.17 | – | – | ++ | ++ | | | 0.42 | 0.071 | 26% | 8.8 |
| Perceived value | . . . | | | | | | | | | | | |
| Ease of assembly | . . . | | | | | | | | | | | |

**Figure 4.11. A Partial QFD Matrix for IKEA**

each service function has on each attribute (as determined by the cross-functional service development team). The relationships are rated on a scale where (+ +) means there is a strong positive relationship; (+), a moderately positive relationship; (–), a moderately negative relationship; and (– –), a strong negative relationship. For example, the team saw a strong positive relationship between having a number of different routes through the store and a customer's ability to browse, but saw a moderately negative relationship between having a number of routes and the experience of a pleasant adventure—more routes increase the feeling of hassle.

Those service qualities or functions that have the greatest effect on the targeted service attributes are themselves targeted for improvement in subsequent QFD stages. Our example shows how functions related to in-store experience are broken down as *quality of paths, showrooms, and exhibits,* and *quality of customer involvement.* These qualities should be as concrete and measurable as possible. This is often difficult in a service context where "measurable" boils down to having customers rate their satisfaction with the qualities.

A good way to organize the service qualities or design functions shown in Figure 4.11 is to create a tree diagram similar to those discussed in Chapter Three. The partial function tree in Figure 4.12 details IKEA's ability to prepare customers for the in-store experience using its website. For the website to become a linked activity for IKEA, it should foster customers' ability to prepare for the self-selection and self-service that occurs in the stores. Two ways in which IKEA performs this activity is through helping customers do their homework and through teaching them how to shop.

Figure 4.12 breaks these two activities down into more concrete tasks, such as how to find a store and navigate it once inside. Breaking these tasks into even more concrete tasks illustrates just how IKEA's website actually works. Figure 4.13 shows an excerpt from IKEA's web pages, which informs customers what to expect from, how to prepare for, and how to navigate an IKEA store.[18] Our goal here is not to provide an exhaustive review of either QFD or IKEA's website design, but rather to show the connection between the design of linked activities and a company's overall service concept. Clearly IKEA's website is designed with its cul-

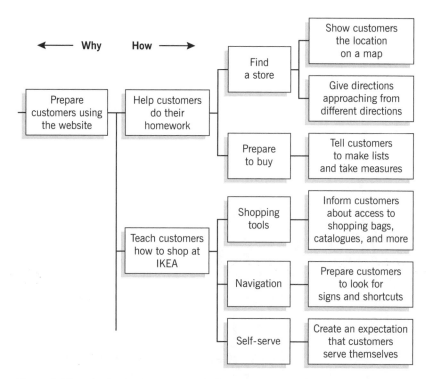

**Figure 4.12.** A Partial Function Tree for IKEA

ture, market segment, and existing linked activities in mind. By understanding how the customer experience impacts satisfaction and loyalty, IKEA can deploy resources to add those links that have the greatest impact on business performance.

## CHAPTER SUMMARY

On the assumption that your service maintenance processes are well established, our goal in Chapter Four has been to raise the bar, improve service performance, and give customers even more reasons to do business with you. Our process for improving service performance comprises four steps: (1) building the lens of the customer, (2) using this lens to collect survey information and model the drivers of customer satisfaction and

your local store
links:
local IKEA jobs
how to prepare
how to shop
how to pay

**bring the kids**

We want everyone to have fun at IKEA, including the kids. That's why we have a children's playroom where your kids can play with others their age. There's only one risk - your kids may have such a good time that they may not want to go home!

**leave the compass at home**

It is actually easy to navigate IKEA stores. Each IKEA store has a clearly marked path that takes you through the entire store. If you are a veteran IKEA-visitor, there are many shortcuts to get you where you want to go quickly. Our helpful, friendly co-workers will be able to assist you.

» store experience

**shopping tools**

When you start shopping, grab a yellow shopping bag to carry your smaller purchases. As you walk through the store you will find catalogues you can borrow, as well as pencils and paper for notes.

Take your time to examine and enjoy the furniture. Try it out, sit in it, lean on it, switch the light on and off. If you don't try it, how will you know if you are going to like it?

**look at the info tag**

This is where that notepaper comes in handy, because on the info tag you will not only find the low price, but also other important facts such as dimensions, country of origin and lots more. Find out more about the remarkable info tag.

» read more

**IKEA saves you money**

Once you are done shopping, you can see for yourself the best part about IKEA - saving money. We ask you to play an active role in retrieving some of your purchases in your store visit. If the products you chose are self-serve items, just go to the self-serve area to pick them up. In return, we pass the savings on to you.

**Figure 4.13. How IKEA's Website Prepares Customers to Shop**

loyalty, (3) using the output of the model to set priorities for quality improvement and innovation, and (4) following through on these priorities using a new service development cycle.

The process starts by using qualitative research to understand your overall service offering from your customers' perspective, what we call the lens of the customer. What are the salient attributes of your offering, and what benefits do they provide customers or what problems do they solve? This lens then can be used to create a blueprint for collecting and analyzing customer perceptions to determine just how well your company performs with respect to the attributes and benefits and what impact they have on satisfaction, loyalty, and profitability. Areas where performance and impact are both high are your sources of competitive advantage. Areas where impact is high yet performance is weak are your competitive vulnerabilities. And by finding completely new ways to improve benefits directly, you tap into new and innovative ways to deepen your competitive service advantage. These priorities for improving service performance serve as input to a new service development cycle, which includes generating new service ideas, evaluating whether these ideas are consistent with your strategy and culture, designing new service concepts, and testing and implementing those concepts.

The most important message of this chapter is that improving service performance is an ongoing process of translating customers' subjective perceptions of performance into ways of improving those perceptions in your organization. No one tool is capable of doing it all. As our case examples illustrate, a combination of tools and processes are needed, from satisfaction and loyalty modeling to planning cycles to QFD. For your service development to elevate itself to the level of true innovation you must integrate customers directly into the process, which is the focus of Chapter Five.

### Questions for Consideration

1. Audit your organization's capability to develop services using the process for improving service performance illustrated in Figure 4.1. Where are your "choke points" in the process? In other words, where does your organization have the most difficulty moving the process forward?

2. How strong is your satisfaction and loyalty measurement system for identifying those service areas in need of improvement? For example, is your system capable of identifying both the impact and performance levels of the attributes and benefits that drive your customers' satisfaction and loyalty?

3. Take a service design concept that your organization is either considering or developing and evaluate it using Tax and Stuart's planning cycle for new service systems. What strengths and weaknesses of the service concept does the analysis reveal?

**5**

# Service Innovation

"Customers are liars! When asked they claim to want the new service. But once we introduce the service, they don't want to pay for it!"

*—A manager in the new service economy*

As co-producers and fellow engineers in the service process, customers are an essential source of new ideas and designs. Whereas product innovation uses customer information as input to an internal process, service innovation should integrate customers directly into the process. Yet as our anonymous quotation suggests, managers have been slow to embrace customers as a source of service ideas. The problem is that far too many companies take a narrow view of customer input. They ask customers superficial questions about what they want and don't want without really understanding the problems that customers face.

Another common problem is that because the "rules of the game have changed," managers rely more on their instincts and feelings. As a result, new services emerge from an ad hoc process and are often unprofitable. Although different from product innovation, service innovation still requires an explicit process to increase the likelihood of developing a service that customers need or want and are willing to pay for, and that your organization can support. This chapter describes a service innovation process that involves customers directly and incorporates the checks and balances required in a service context. We illustrate the process using recent service development projects from the airline and telecommunication industries.

### ■ Innovation in a Broader Context

Service innovations are not new to the world, but they may still be new to your company, customers, or network partners. For example, when GE developed its jet engine maintenance service, customers were already performing maintenance functions on their own or within a network of service providers. GE simply took ownership over more of the overall service process.

Service innovations often force a company to work in totally different ways. This is one reason why many product and service companies find service innovation difficult. When things are going well it's hard to "rock the boat" and take the organization in what may be perceived as new directions. Yet the difficulty can be made more manageable if service innovation is viewed in a broader, unifying context of building the culture, staying focused, and linking activities. Maintaining or improving existing links while simultaneously developing new links should be viewed as related, ongoing activities.

The service maintenance, improvement, and development processes we described in Chapters Three and Four are mainly defensive in nature. They remove things gone wrong and build on things gone right in order to satisfy and retain existing customers. Service innovation is inherently more offensive. While helping you keep old customers, innovation also brings new customers into your portfolio. But many companies fail because of their inability to play both defense and offense simultaneously—defending old business and pursuing new ideas.[1]

Figure 5.1 illustrates how our hierarchy of service development is an ongoing process that is constantly working to both protect and grow your competitive service advantage and customer portfolio. Each service that you offer has its own life cycle. As is true of a new technology, once a new service is introduced the unexpected is bound to happen. Things will go wrong! The service will require maintenance in order to make it more reliable. As the service matures and reliability improves, customers

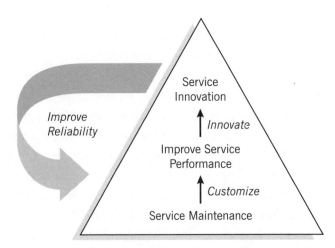

**Figure 5.1.** Natural Progression of the Service Development Hierarchy

expect you to customize the service to better fit the needs of particular market segments. Eventually customers expect customization to their own individual needs. As any existing service can only be customized so much, you eventually innovate your business as the market changes. We shall, for example, discuss how self-service technologies enhance or replace human interaction to facilitate customization.

Our point is that you can't be content to focus on any one stage of the service development hierarchy. Looking across your entire service concept or set of linked activities, you will see that some require improved reliability, others improved customization, and still others innovation. In Chapter One we described how your stages of cultural, service, and customer evolution dictate where to start. When reliability problems threaten your core business, start by improving reliability! When your strategy dictates moving downstream in the value chain to offer value-added services, innovate! But over time you should find yourself active at all levels of the hierarchy.

## ■ Our Service Innovation Process

Innovation is a process rather than an event and must be managed as such.[2] Innovation doesn't just happen. It is the result of deliberate and focused activities that aim to accomplish something new. Don't confuse innovation with invention. An invention is but the first step in a long process of bringing a good idea to widespread and effective use. Companies with brilliant ideas succeed in building a good business because they execute a strategy to make things happen. Thus the whole process of service innovation depends on finding and developing creative ideas.

Research suggests that between 35 and 44 percent of all new services and products fail.[3] This underscores the need to think differently about innovations than about current offerings. You must ensure that the new service corresponds to a need that is important and valuable enough that customers are willing to pay for it. Innovation is inherently risky, and even well-endowed firms cannot take unlimited risks. It is essential that (1) some choices be made among the various market and technology opportunities, (2) these choices fit within your overall business strategy, (3) the choices build on established areas of technical and marketing competence, and, last but not least, (4) your organization works directly with customers along the way. Figure 5.2 summarizes a structured approach to accomplishing these goals. In the sections that follow we describe each stage of the process in detail.

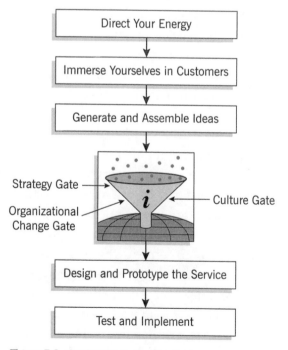

**Figure 5.2. Our Service Innovation Process**

## Direct Your Energy

Service innovation is a double-edged sword of problems and opportunities. The opportunities potentially canvass your entire value chain. The problem is to direct your energy to those parts of the chain that are consistent with your overall corporate or organizational strategy and resources (such as financial and technological resources and the strength of your brand, reputation, and customer relationships). A natural way to start looking for opportunities is by scanning the environment for fundamental industry changes, such as new technology opportunities, new moves by competitors, and changing market, business, or legal conditions.

Scanning the environment may reveal possibilities for innovation that result from the interplay of multiple forces. For instance, many new services are made possible by the combination of new technology and a customer base seeking to serve itself at its own convenience. These innovations take the form of self-service technologies that enable customers to produce services themselves without any direct involvement or interaction with a firm's employees.[4] These might include on-line bill paying and account management services and customer relationship management (CRM) systems that allow customers to access information that previously required service personnel (such as downloading service tips or software from Dell or tax forms and instructions from the Internal Revenue Service).

Self-service technology is particularly applicable in a business-to-consumer (B-to-C) context where one-to-one marketing is difficult because the customer base is large. It provides scalability: the ability to quickly and cost-effectively scale an operation up from relatively few to many customers. Such scalability has helped companies such as Charles Schwab and Amazon enhance their customer value propositions. The new technology can be accessed round the clock and rarely calls in sick or takes a holiday. Customers can access the service from practically any-where at any time and have more control over the interaction. Although overall service remains a primarily human interaction, not all customers enjoy meeting employees, which is another reason why self-service technology can be advantageous.

Richard Normann offers the following questions to help you explore opportunities for self-service technology:[5]

Is it possible to influence when your customers need the service?

Is your customers' waiting time wasted time?

Do service personnel and customers meet face-to-face unneces-sarily?

Are face-to-face contacts being leveraged as much as they could be?

Is it possible to transfer some of the repetitive tasks that your employees perform to customers using the technology?

Are customers trying to bypass the employees and perform part of the service themselves?

Is it possible to leverage this interest and knowledge?

Do customers display an interest in what your service person-nel are doing?

Do a few customers interfere with the service system and make it less effective?

Are customers asking for information that is available else-where?

Is it possible to move part of the service processes in order to use costly space more effectively?

Is it possible for customers to choose between different service levels?

Although the answers to these questions might direct you to use more self-service technology, keep in mind that by walk-ing down the technology path too far you run the risk of be-coming a commodity service supplier competing on price. Over time, the technology will be easier to copy than a strong customer service culture and the linked activities it supports. How, for example, can you create a close relationship with customers just using the Internet? Another hazard is that not all of your customers feel comfortable using self-service technologies. Parasuraman's research on the Technology Readiness Index (TRI) shows systematic differences across customer segments with respect to their attitudes toward technology and resulting propensity to embrace and employ technology.[6]

In business-to-business (B-to-B) applications the problem is somewhat different, as suppliers are probably adding services to an existing product offering. The goals here are to understand just what your business customers have to go through to do business with you and focus on removing "points of pain." What costs can be removed to make life easier for them, and can you perform the activities more cost-effectively or better than others? Recall from Chapter One how SPC examined the entire life cycle of its products' purchase, use, and disposal to identify opportunities for developing a set of linked IT-based service activities (including an order entry service, technical expertise, and railcar tracking service).

The SPC case underscores another important industry trend identified in Chapter One—product-to-service transformations. Viewing products as services waiting to happen changes your mind-set from production to usage, from products to processes, and from transactions to relationships. As more and more of the profit margins in business are downstream in the value chain, manufacturing companies will continue to move in that direction. William Clay Ford Jr., president and CEO of Ford Motor Company, describes the trend in the automotive industry:

> If you go back to even a very short while ago, our whole idea of a customer was that we would wholesale a car to a dealer, the dealer would then sell the car to the customer, and we

hoped we never heard from the customer—because if we did, it meant something was wrong. Today we want to establish a dialogue with the customer throughout the entire ownership experience. We want to talk to and touch our customers at every step of the way. We want to be a consumer products and services company that just happens to be in the automotive business. The Internet is key to all of this.[7]

So, where should you direct your energy? We won't pretend to tell you where along the value chain to focus. That depends on your overall strategy of what business you want to be in and how you want to compete. To provide some guidance, Figure 5.3 takes a fairly high-level look at the value chain from a services perspective. We divide the chain into four categories: (1) business model, (2) service support activities, (3) customer service activities, and (4) customer outcomes. The latter three categories correspond to Edvardsson's service logic model, described in Chapter Four.

Rethinking your service business model forces you to address some of the questions we just explored. How much of your

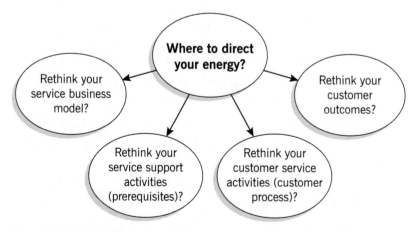

**Figure 5.3. Where to Direct Your Energy?**

service should involve human interaction versus technology? How much should your value proposition depend on products versus services? And how transaction oriented versus relationship oriented should you be? Rethinking your service support activities involves reevaluating those linked activities that are prerequisites for providing a service such as IKEA's low-cost manufacturing and in-house design. Rethinking your customer service activities means looking to those linked activities that directly involve the customer, such as how customers use catalogues or the Web to prepare themselves to shop at IKEA. Rethinking customer outcomes might include changing branding or relationship management activities to enhance the ultimate customer experience, as when IKEA offers customers free cooking and home decoration classes. These activities help IKEA build relationships with its customers in between those times when customers are buying furniture or housewares.

### Immerse Yourselves in Customers

Having set your sights on where to innovate, the next step is to immerse yourselves in customers. The goal is to gain a comprehensive understanding of the problems customers have to solve, the experiences they are trying to achieve, and why. You won't necessarily gain this understanding by talking to managers or employees or buying market research reports or consulting services. You should have direct access to customers to understand their underlying needs and values. Reading reports or seeing presentations is no substitute for experiencing exactly what your customers have to go through. A deep understanding of your customers should become a core competency.

This requires moving beyond traditional market and customer research methods and tools. Focus groups, CIT, and questionnaires require some previous experience on which customers can reflect. Of course, customers have no previous experience with a service that is entirely new. More often than not, service innovation involves observing and probing to understand just what customers are trying to accomplish when using a product or service, and finding new ways to help them accomplish their goals. The tools and methods described in Chapters Three and Four are important and useful when eliminating defects and improving customization. But they are reactive—they focus on existing problems and opportunities with an existing service.

There are various proactive market research methods aimed at understanding customers' underlying needs and values. Keep in mind that these methods won't provide the answers or innovations per se, but rather the information required to develop them. Here we discuss six such methods: (1) research into history and fundamental national factors, (2) unobtrusive measures and observations, (3) value segmentation, (4) comparing noncomparables, (5) projective techniques, and (6) means-end chain analysis.[8] Other methods described elsewhere include trend extrapolation and scenario development.[9]

*History and National Factors*
History and fundamental national factors establish basic differences among countries and cultures. The primary information source is history and research on cultural differences. If your company wants to launch a new service in a new country, you certainly need to know how customers in the country are likely to accept and use your service. A good example of the usefulness of cross-cultural comparisons comes from Hofstede's research, in which nations are measured on four descriptive dimensions: power distance (the extent to which inequality is accepted), individualism (the extent of self- versus collective interest), masculinity (well-defined versus overlapping sex roles), and uncertainty avoidance (acceptance of "unstructured, unclear, or unpredictable" situations).[10] This research has shown that people in the United States place greater value on power distance

and individualism than do people in Sweden. These differences suggest that Web or media-based services designed to promote individual accomplishments have a higher likelihood of success in the United States.

### Unobtrusive Measures and Observations

Unobtrusive or nonreactive measures include a wide range of physical trace, archival, and observational information. This information is collected without customers being explicitly aware they are being measured. As CRM systems become increasingly sophisticated, customers leave tracks that can be studied and used to develop new services. We illustrate the use of observation near the end of the chapter in a case study from SAS.

### Value Segmentation

Value segmentation clusters customers with similar root values, defined as customers' enduring beliefs. For instance, some people regard their family life as more important than their career goals, and vice versa. These root values are identified using surveys that make no mention of particular products or services. Figure 5.4 illustrates how Ericsson, a global telecommunications

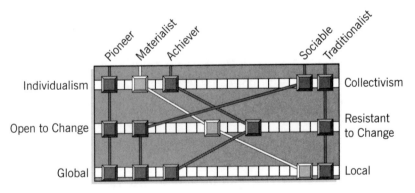

**Figure 5.4.** One of Ericsson's Segmentation Models

company, used customer values to develop its segmentation scheme. Ericsson classifies customers as pioneers, achievers, materialists, sociables, or traditionalists based on how they rate themselves on three dimensions: (1) individualism versus collectivism, (2) openness versus resistance to change, and (3) global versus local perspective. The company has used the research to understand that its primary customers are achievers (well-educated career people working with high-tech products yet resistant to change). The information has helped Ericsson understand how the attitudes and behavior of this segment change and which innovations are most appropriate. Another common proxy for value or lifestyle segmentation is the use of postal codes to segment people where geographically based lifestyle differences are well documented.

### Comparing Noncomparables

Comparing noncomparables involves asking respondents to compare totally different products, services, or companies for their similarities and differences. One might ask a customer to compare his banker with his broker. He responds that whereas the banker is more accessible and friendly, the broker is a better source of market knowledge. Such information provides the banker or broker with a better idea of how to compete for the customer's financial services.

### Projective Techniques

Projective techniques are a way to avoid eliciting socially acceptable or status quo responses from customers during interviews, focus groups, or surveys. They ask respondents to project their feelings or attitudes toward a product or service indirectly onto a third party. For example, respondents might be given descriptions of one of two shoppers who are identical with respect to age, income, education, ethnic background, and where they shop for groceries. The only difference between the shoppers is that one buys furniture and housewares from IKEA and the other has items shipped from mail-order catalogues. Projecting their attitudes and beliefs onto the two descriptions, customers might describe the first shopper as thrifty and hard working and the second as a lazy spendthrift.

*Means-End Chain Analysis*
Means-end chain analysis involves asking customers why a given product or service attribute is important to them. What benefits or values does the attribute serve, or what problems or consequences does it create? The interviewer continues to probe the customer for answers until he or she can no longer answer because the root need or value has been reached. The product or service attributes are the means, and the personal values are the ends. Means-end theory seeks to explain how a person's choice of a product or service enables him or her to achieve desired end states. For example, faster and more reliable service at the bank saves customers time, which allows them to be more efficient and thus increases their sense of accomplishment—the ultimate goal. We employed a variation on this approach in our CIT methodology discussed in Chapters Three and Four, probing customers to understand the benefits and consequences of their service "likes" and "dislikes."

On the whole, these more proactive research methods provide an understanding of your customers' root needs and values that is an excellent basis for innovation. The methods help you think outside your current product or service offering and focus more on the problems customers are trying to solve and the root needs and values they are trying to serve.

## Generate and Assemble Ideas

The next step in the innovation process is to generate and assemble new service ideas. *Are your customers active participants in this process?* If not, you are probably ignoring one of your best and most underutilized sources of creativity. Innovations based on ideas from customers are more likely to lead to market success than those based on technology alone.[11] Research by Eric von Hippel finds that users themselves invent, prototype, and use most physical goods before those goods are ever offered by commercial firms.[12] Unfortunately, our experience is that managers and researchers largely ignore customers' new service ideas. Granted there are some ways in which customers make poor contributors. They often don't have a good overall picture of your linked activities or target market. They don't know what is technically possible to accomplish and may have hidden motives. Yet as "engineers" in the service process who are unencumbered by your organization and its constraints, customers are more likely to think "outside the box" and develop ideas that meet their needs.

Leveraging customers as a resource requires a structured process that allows them to contribute. You will find it difficult to engage just any old customer in the creative process; some are simply unwilling or unable to get involved. Others are intimidated or worried that you will learn too much about them. But if you succeed in engaging customers in the process, they can contribute through their experiences, knowledge, skills, willingness to learn and experiment, and ability to take part in an active dialogue. By directly involving customers in your innovation process you stand to lower development costs and create services that both are easier to use and have a higher likelihood of market acceptance. The key is to have an explicit process for generating and assembling customers' ideas, which we illustrate later in the chapter using a recent study from the telecom industry.

### The Strategy, Culture, and Organizational Change Gates

Once you have developed and assembled ideas from customers and other sources, the third step in the innovation process is to select those ideas for development that have the greatest potential for success. Both product and service development typically include a funneling process at this point, in which ideas pass through a series of checkpoints or stage gates. But services differ from products in the nature of the gates. Our model for building a competitive service advantage (introduced in Chapter Two) emphasizes two essential checkpoints—the strategy and culture gates. These same two gates apply to the process of innovation. You need to make sure that new service ideas are consistent with your overall service strategy and its linked activities. If they are, you then need to ensure that your customer service culture and norms can support the strategy-consistent ideas.

As service innovations are more likely to be new to the organization, we add a third checkpoint for innovation. Ask, If the innovation is not completely consistent with our culture, can our organization change its culture to accommodate the innovation? We have emphasized throughout this book just how important a stable culture is to service success. But we don't mean that the culture can be static, myopic, or completely resistant to change. Company culture may be your biggest advantage or disadvantage. Companies frequently get locked into their own business models and become reluctant to change their technology, products, services, or distribution channels. They focus on providing what customers wanted yesterday. You can't jump on every idea that comes along. But you have to be open to change. As Tushman and O'Reilly note, "Culture is key both to short-term success and, unless managed correctly, to long-term failure. Culture can provide competitive advantage, but it can also create obstacles to the innovation and change necessary to be successful."[13]

Steve Case, chairman and CEO of America Online, describes AOL's success in these terms:

I think one of the things that served this company well over these past fifteen years was that we weren't wedded to any prior culture. If we had grown up in Silicon Valley, we probably would have looked at the world through the prism of technology. If we would have been born in Hollywood, the prism would have been entertainment. If we started in Basking Ridge, New Jersey [where AT&T is headquartered], we would have seen ourselves as a communication company. It's not possible for most companies to put aside decades or sometimes a century of traditions and lessons learned and not apply it in the future. Sometimes that's helpful, because you avoid making the same mistakes over again. But most of the time it's harmful, because you end up assuming that the future is going to look like the past—which in the case of our industry it usually isn't. AOL grew up in northern Virginia, where there was really no culture, just a sleepy government town with lots of government contractors. We started from scratch.[14]

### Following Through

The last two steps in the service innovation process are service design and prototyping followed by testing and implementation. These steps are similar to those detailed in Chapter Four. Customer involvement is also important at these stages, and particularly useful for the rapid prototyping that is common in a manufacturing setting. The rapid prototyping of services involves having customers pilot-test service prototypes and provide feedback, and improving the prototypes until they earn customer approval. This effectively combines aspects of service testing with service design and prototyping to reduce time to market and increase the likelihood of success. By providing feedback during the development stages, customers become co-designers of the service. Microsoft effectively used this type of beta-testing and feedback in the development of its Windows 2000 operating system.[15] Telia Mobile used the process to develop its initial Unified Messaging service that integrated its e-mail, fax, and voice mail services.

Here's a warning. It is often at these final stages of the innovation process that paralysis sets in. Managers and employees get stuck in processes and routines that have worked well in the past. We hear three common phrases: (1) "This is the way we have always done it," (2) "We have never done it that way before," and (3) "It may work for them but not for us—we're special!" We can't tell you how to respond to such comments—that depends on your company and context. But you should be ready for them.

The next two sections of the chapter are cases that illustrate the service innovation process in action. The first shows how SAS immersed itself in customers to develop creative service ideas and designs.[16] The second shows how a large telecommunications company used customers to generate more innovative and user-friendly ideas.

### Innovation Through Observation at SAS

Airline travelers are routinely forced into a system characterized by contradictions, redundant or insufficient information, misguided authority, and confusion. They are expected to carry out or participate in a series of activities, each of which individually might seem logical but when taken together lead to an impression of chaos. Uncertainties often dominate the system, which results in a sense of randomness that overwhelms even the most experienced of travelers.

Realizing the possible gains for the company that succeeds in reformulating the fundamental concept of air travel, SAS made a strategic decision to become an innovation leader. Working with the Doblin Group, a Chicago-based innovation and strategy firm, SAS sought to rethink its customer service activities (customer process).[17] An important step in turning this strategy into reality was to develop a thorough understanding of the spoken and unspoken needs and expectations of its customers. SAS asked itself a relatively simple question: *What do customers actually do when they travel?* Though SAS employees and managers were spending every working day watching what customers do, they often got lost in routines and existing processes and didn't see what was really important to customers.

SAS studied customers in environments across the entire air travel process. Studies were carried out partly by using direct observation, but foremost by using video to document the customers' travel process. Video monitors and cameras were installed in a wide variety of locations. In all, SAS amassed thousands of hours of video and photographic data of the customers on the ground and in-flight. The visual data were then analyzed to identify recurring passenger needs and concerns. Close to fifteen hundred hours of video data were studied in sequences as short as five seconds. This conscientious analysis of video data formed the basis for an understanding of passengers and how they perceive different activities. The travel experience was divided into the five phases shown in Figure 5.5: check-in, lounge, gate, in-flight, and baggage claim. Each phase roughly represents a physical location or a function that passengers pass through as they interact with SAS.

For each of the five phases, customer activities—both voluntary and those prescribed by the travel system—were closely examined. A walk through the halls of an airport quickly reveals that passengers do not engage in a single, focused activity. Whether they are in line to board, searching for a gate, or waiting for a colleague, the combination of flight-oriented events and the complexity of everyday life produces a seemingly endless variety of activities. Less obvious to the eye but apparent through analysis of video data were general patterns underlying the myriad activities. SAS systematized the activities and focused on clusters of similar customer behaviors. In this way it was able to identify three broad categories of activity: (1) procedural, (2) personal, and (3) planning and

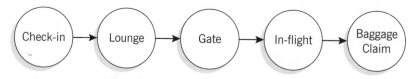

**Figure 5.5.** The Travel Experience as a Customer Service Process

preparation. Procedural activities follow from all the rules and regulations that surround air travel. The rules and regulations require passengers to perform a number of activities with a certain degree of success in order to be allowed to travel. Personal activities consist of all the things that everyday life demands, even while people are constrained within the travel experience. Planning and preparation activities arise because both procedural and personal activities demand measures of planning and preparation.

Each of the general categories was then subdivided. For instance, the procedural activities were divided into two subcategories: exchanging value and navigating. Exchanging value refers to the system of giving and receiving that takes place as passengers progress through the travel experience. For example, in exchange for a boarding pass the passenger is allowed to pass through a guarded doorway to the plane. Customers often misunderstand this peddling of papers, regarding it as unnecessary and bureaucratic. Navigating represents the activities needed to progress through the many environments and procedures.

From the video data it was obvious that many customers had great difficulty figuring out where to go and, perhaps even more important, what to do during different phases of the travel experience. One frequent observation was the navigational chaos involved when finding one's seat and storing luggage. Where else but on an airplane do people jostle for space in such close quarters without (usually) coming to blows? Two other frequent observations were the challenge and mystery associated with eating a snack or meal. The challenge is to enjoy the snack in a cramped space. The mystery is to identify what one is about to eat.

By identifying the abundance of activities that occur throughout the travel experience and detecting the underlying patterns and structures that guide these activities, SAS developed a more thorough understanding of its customers' needs and expectations. From this understanding it was able to create a set of detailed development guidelines to support the different activity categories and to define new service concepts within each activity cluster.

If one were working solely with the extensive results from the study, however, it would be difficult to prioritize the development guidelines and choose which new service concepts to pursue. SAS needed some rules of thumb or design principles that would help direct its energy strategically. For this, the video data proved to be a priceless source of information, allowing SAS to identify places where the company wasn't focusing on customers. These insights led SAS to articulate three design principles, shown in Figure 5.6: give passengers control, make the process transparent, and empower the staff.

The study revealed how rules, regulations, and SAS's own systems were influencing its services. It showed customers trying to carry out personal activities while being treated like luggage that is inspected, tagged, and sent on its way. SAS could also see that passengers were being forced to resort to unconventional solutions (such as bringing their own food on the plane) in order to get through the process (recall the hierarchy of SAS customer needs discussed in Chapter Two). It was vital that SAS succeed in engaging customers in the travel experience and letting them decide for themselves what level of support they needed. SAS had to provide passengers with information that would empower them and allow them to serve themselves through their journey and give them the freedom to take an active part in creating the travel experience. In this way SAS could give its customers control over their own experience.

Using the findings from the study, the development guidelines, and the design principles, SAS prioritized three main areas of innovation in the following order: (1) in-flight services, (2) ground services, and (3) information services. In-flight services and ground services more or less correspond to the different phases of the travel experience, whereas information services serve as a fabric connecting the phases and binding them together. Keeping these three areas in mind allowed SAS to create a series of linked activities that are difficult for competitors to imitate. For example, SAS installed kiosks in their hubs that allow customers not only to

**Figure 5.6.** Prioritized Design Principles

interact with SAS but also to use the Web to book meals and further travel and to get news and weather information.

Another outcome of the design and prototyping phases of SAS's service innovation process was the Gate Café concept, developed in response to the formation of "huddled masses" prior to the boarding of airline flights. The idea was to create separate self-service food areas for both economy and Euroclass flyers. The sketches in Figure 5.7 illustrate the Gate Café concept. Feeding passengers during the waiting process makes them less anxious to board the plane as fast as possible. Separating the different classes of passengers facilitates queuing, allowing the Euroclass flyers to board at their leisure. Allowing passengers to eat before boarding or to take only that food on the plane that they want reduces the complexity of services that need to be offered on board. Passengers

**Figure 5.7.** The Gate Café Concept

appreciate being able to pick out their own food and having clear knowledge of what they are eating.

The events of September 11, 2001, have slowed the pace of innovation at SAS, as it and other airlines made safety and capacity utilization their top concerns. However, as industry conditions improve, SAS will continue to test and implement service innovations that help customers through the travel process, link activities, and create a competitive service advantage.

## The Value of User Ideas at Telia Mobile

How valuable is it to directly involve customers in the service innovation process? The following case study is based on research conducted by Per Kristensson and Jonas Matthing of the Service Research Center at Karlstad University and Peter Magnusson of the Stockholm School of Economics.[18] The research was conducted for Telia Mobile, a large Swedish telecommunications company. Inspired by a methodology called lead user,[19] the purpose of the study was to examine whether customers or companies are better at identifying and expressing needs and developing ideas.

**The Research Design and Procedure.**  As subjects for the study, sixty-eight men and women were assigned to the following four groups:

1. Twelve professional participants from the telecommunications company, who served as *company experts*
2. Sixteen customers identified as *lead users*
3. Nineteen customers classified as *ordinary customers* who would work on their own during the study
4. Twenty-one people also classified as *ordinary customers* but who would interact *with company experts* during the study (not the same company experts as in the first group)

The company experts worked as service developers in the R&D department of Telia Mobile. The lead users were customers with computer science backgrounds. The fourth group was formed to allow the researchers to observe customers and company experts working together (asking questions of each other and discussing possibilities and ideas).

The development context was the design of a collection of mobile phone services based on a technology called GSM standard SMS (the abbreviation for Global System for Mobile telecommunications standard Short Message Service). The service platform used in the study was called Unified Services (US). What US essentially does is convert SMS messages (text messages in the mobile phone) into GSM and http calls on the Internet. US enables a person to access information on the Internet by sending and receiving SMS messages. It also allows for remote control of certain devices. For example, it creates a service that can switch the lights or the heating system in your home on and off or that can check to see if your doors are locked.

It was important to engage customers in the task within an explicit process or procedure by which their ideas could be properly captured, evaluated, and compared with the ideas put forth by the experts. As shown in Figure 5.8, the procedure started with the recruitment of users and ended with the evaluation of ideas. At an initial meeting for the customers involved in the study, those conducting the study described the toolkit (the US application platform) to provide participants with a feeling of the range of possibilities for this kind of service. Then all participants (experts, lead users, and ordinary customers) were equipped with mobile phones and a platform for mobile Internet that they could take home. They were each given the task of developing and, if possible, implement-

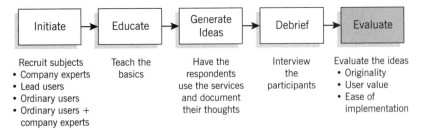

**Figure 5.8.** The Research Procedure

ing new service ideas that would add customer value. The idea was that having the necessary equipment in their home environment would encourage the participants to develop completely new ideas. The company experts' task was to develop new service ideas for customers; the customers' task was to develop new service ideas for themselves.

All participants were instructed to document the idea creation process in a diary, the purpose being to collect process data and record ideas as they emerged. To give participants a better sense of how new services could work, they were given access to a sample of ten services that had already been implemented. To enable participants to test these services and to inspire them during the experiment, the mobile telephone was loaded with a prepaid card (cash value of approximately $25) and a "chat-board." All participants received hands-on training on how to use the phone and chat-board.

In the third phase, each of the participants worked for twelve days to develop new ideas and solutions to the presented problems. On the third day, the researchers checked in with each participant via the mobile phones. Throughout the idea generation period, participants were instructed to individually report any problems in their diary. The toolkit and a help desk were at their service throughout. After twelve days, the idea generation period ended, and respondents were debriefed. Participants returned all equipment and were asked to write down, using a standardized service description format, descriptions of the service ideas that they had come up with. These service descriptions were the subject of the evaluation process.

A consensual assessment technique (CAT) was then employed to evaluate the ideas. CAT uses a panel of independent judges to compare different ideas and designs, judge them relative to each other, and rank them. Different expert panels of three judges each were used to evaluate the ideas. One panel was made up of *industry experts,* technical consultants from outside the company who were experts in the telecommunication industry. Another panel was of *marketing staff,* employees from Telia's marketing area. A third panel was of *ordinary customers.* A fourth panel was of *company experts,* technically skilled product developers from Telia's R&D department who, along with the industry experts, were asked to evaluate ease of implementation within the company.

**Are Customers' Ideas Really Better?** The experiment yielded 362 new service ideas. Each of the ideas was judged on 10-point scales for originality, user value, and ease of implementation. Figure 5.9 shows the average scores for originality by source according to the evaluations of three different panels. Ordinary customers developed the most original ideas, followed by customers and company experts working together, company experts, and lead users respectively. The lower scores for the company experts and lead users are particularly interesting. The explanation is that these experts tended to focus more narrowly on what was possible to accomplish today rather than in the future. Also interesting is that when ordinary customers were tutored by company experts, originality decreased.

The average scores for user value, shown in Figure 5.10, show the same general pattern. The best ideas came from the ordinary customers followed by the ordinary customers working with experts, the lead users, and the company experts. Thus customers developed more original and useful SMS service ideas. But after all, who's in a better position to generate ideas than customers themselves? As simple as this idea is, we continue to be surprised by the number of companies and managers who

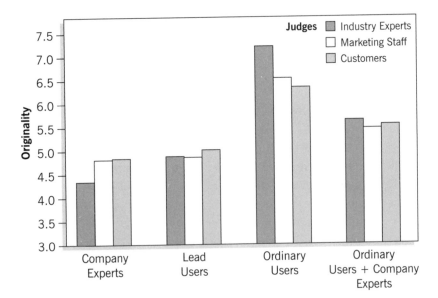

**Figure 5.9. Originality Scores**

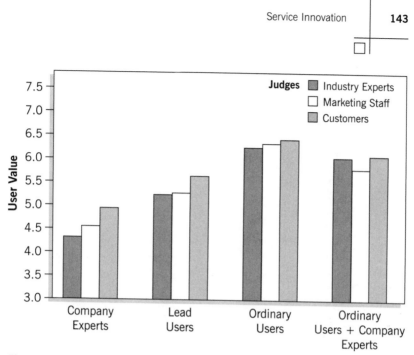

**Figure 5.10.** User Value Scores

are unwilling to leverage customer creativity and knowledge in service development.

Finally, it is interesting to see how industry experts rated the ease of implementation of the ideas (see Figure 5.11). You might think that the ordinary customers' ideas would suffer on this dimension, but that is clearly not the case. If anything, customers' ideas appear easier to implement as well.

The differences between the ratings of company and industry experts in Figure 5.11 are worth examining. Ease of implementation could be judged only by these two groups (service developers from the company's R&D department and technical consultants from outside the company). Company experts rate their own ideas the easiest to implement; industry experts rate lead users' ideas highest on this dimension. Industry experts also rate the company experts' ideas relatively low on ease of implementation. It appears that company experts overestimated the ease of implementation of their own ideas.

Overall the results speak for themselves. Ordinary users were clearly the best source of creative ideas. One customer-generated idea was to be

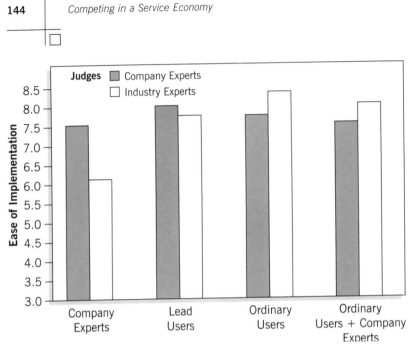

**Figure 5.11.** Ease of Implementation Scores

able to use a cell phone to quickly remind a newspaper delivery person that he had forgotten to leave a paper. Still another was to use the cell phone to geographically locate one's children at the mall. The lesson is that if you are not including ordinary customers directly in your service development process, you are probably making a big mistake. Not only do customers have better ideas, implying that you will improve quality by including them in the process, but you may also save money by relying on their competence.

## CHAPTER SUMMARY

Service innovation is more than just asking customers what they want. It's an explicit process of deciding where to direct your energy, immersing yourselves in customers' lives, and working with customers to generate, design, and test new ideas. Service innovation is an essential part of your overall service development effort. Once a service is made reliable and customized to market segment or individual needs, innovation paves the way to develop completely new ways to solve customer problems, serve customers' values, and attract new customers.

Just where you should direct your energy depends on whether you need to rethink your business model, your service support activities, your customer service activities, or your desired customer outcomes. Immersing yourselves in customers' lives requires going beyond such traditional market and customer research methods as interviews, focus groups, and surveys, which typically focus on what customers are already familiar with. Rather, it requires observing and probing to understand just what customers are trying to accomplish or what problems they are trying to solve. Observational methods, value surveys, and other proactive methods give you a better understanding of your customers' root needs and values and an excellent basis for innovation. As fellow engineers in the service process, customers are unencumbered by your organization and its constraints. Taking advantage of this and making customers active participants in your innovation process require a structured approach that allows them to contribute and documents their ideas.

We've seen how SAS uses proactive research to develop a deep understanding of their customers' travel experience and use this understanding to design new concepts and prototypes. Our study of idea generation in the telecom industry shows how customers develop the most original and useful service ideas in the day-to-day course of their lives. In the final chapter of our book, we look across all our frameworks, processes, and case studies to see what we've learned along the way about the role of leaders in a service company.

## Questions for Consideration

1. Where does your organization need to direct its energy in order to innovate through services?
2. Of the different proactive research methods described in the chapter (history and national factors, observation, value surveys and segmentation, comparing noncomparables, projective techniques, and means-end chain analysis), which method or methods do you believe would help your organization better understand its customers' needs?
3. Using the Telia Mobile case as an example, what concrete process or approach could you implement to help capture customers' ideas as a source of service innovation?

# Lead the Way

W e began this saga with a simple observation: *economies are more service based than ever!* Competitive forces continue to push you to provide customers with more than just product value. Increasingly it's service value, solutions, and experiences that differentiate competitors. Whether you are managing a traditional service organization or a manufacturing firm, competing through services has become a way of life. From our discussion and research into service strategies, maintenance, improvement, and innovation we can extract some important lessons regarding the role of leaders in the process. It is fitting to end our exploration by sharing these insights with you. Here again we will follow our framework for creating a competitive service advantage: build the culture, stay focused, and link activities. We will also bring back a familiar character from earlier chapters, IKEA's Ingvar Kamprad, and hear from Disney's Michael Eisner.

## ■ Are You Building the Culture?

*Live the culture!* Remember that your organizational culture serves as the basis for a more specific customer service culture. This culture drives your strategy decisions, the activities that you link and for whom, and your ability to execute a differentiated service offering and provide it to customers. At IKEA the underlying cultural values of thrift, inventiveness, and hard work support a customer service culture in which customers are an integral part of the co-production process. As part of the IKEA family, they contribute by selecting, transporting, assembling, and even advertising the furniture and housewares themselves. It is essential that employees and customers see company leaders who live the company's values, as opposed to those who just communicate them through memos and presentations.

A store manager recently told us a story that exemplifies how Ingvar Kamprad continues to live and reinforce the IKEA culture. The company recently opened its first Chinese store locations in Beijing and Shanghai. Early one day, the management of the Beijing store were completely surprised to see Kamprad enter the store. Then he spent the whole day walking the floor with the management and staff to see for himself how things were going. He wasn't there to tell people what to do or how to do it. Rather, he offered some ideas and patiently explained the history and logic of IKEA's business practices (its linked activities). When it came time to leave, the store manager offered to take him out to dinner and drive him back to his hotel. Kamprad politely refused, preferring to go back to his hotel the same way he came, using public transportation. Like the "many people," Kamprad simply took the bus. To the staff of the Beijing store this exemplified and reinforced everything they had been taught about the "IKEA way."

*Manage by walking around!* Kamprad's visit to the store in China illustrates another important trait of service leaders. They spend as much time as possible in the service setting interacting with both employees and customers. A service organization is a collection of human beings. It is impossible to understand your people, much less have them live the culture, unless you are right there with them. Michael Eisner, chairman and CEO of Disney, emphasizes the difficulty of "being there" as an organization grows. "If you have an organization that is small enough, being there simply means having contact and exposure and being available. When the organization gets bigger, it is unbelievably frustrating to a leader that you can't be there for everyone."[1]

How do service leaders manage the problems associated with growth? Larger service and retail companies develop leadership teams. Each linked activity, brand, or franchise has its own leader who can live the culture and manage by walking around. Business leaders and service researchers often talk about the importance of thinking big while acting small. Managing by walking around is an essential part of the process. Indeed, the beginning of the end is when you start to think of your company as a big one.

*Focus on employees!* Remember that how you treat your employees determines how they'll treat your customers. Services are, after all, highly individual and personal experiences. Acting small with customers means having your employees go purposely out of their way to treat customers personally.[2] The key to creating an effective customer service culture is treating your employees with respect, deferring to their experience, and creating a fun place to work. As Berry concludes, "Humane organizational values such as joy, teamwork, and respect; a shared vision of high purpose; and an emphasis on organizational trust, 'relationship employees,' and employee ownership attitudes all contribute to an intimate, collaborative work environment that encourages human excellence."[3] Excellent service leaders and their employees manage to have fun even as the organization grows. As Disney's Eisner explains, "Maybe we don't whistle while we work, but we do smile and tell jokes. Of course, that kind of culture doesn't just happen—you have to make it happen."[4]

### ■ Are Your Activities Linked?

*Manage all levels of service development simultaneously!* Service leaders are marked by their constant pursuit of service maintenance, service performance, and service innovation. One of the major traps that we see executives of any business fall into is the "tennis match" phenomenon. Just as a tennis ball is played back and forth over the net between two players, so are company initiatives played back and forth between two competing emphases: reducing costs versus generating revenue. Rather than pursing them as parallel activities, too many companies periodically emphasize improving productivity and lowering costs until they eventually rediscover the need to better understand their customers, innovate, and generate revenues. Excellent companies have a portfolio of services and product technologies that they manage and improve constantly, whether at the innovation stage, the maintenance stage, or the performance improvement stage.

Service companies in particular need to focus on all three activities simultaneously because that is how to build a competitive service advantage. For product companies, it is more important to focus on those activities that support core competencies—for example, Honda's capabilities in engine design and production. For a service organization, we have emphasized how differentiation comes not from doing any one thing better than competitors but from linking an entire network of activities. A differentiated service organization is like a machine in which new parts (new service activities) are constantly being added to essential old parts. These new activities cannot be added without simultaneously maintaining or improving the performance of your existing service activities.

*Emphasize creativity and spontaneity!* As the leader of a service organization, you are not the only one with great ideas. It is essential that you view your employees and customers as sources of creativity and innovation. You should emphasize creativity and spontaneity as cultural norms on a daily basis. For example, IKEA refers to the "Testament of a Furniture Dealer," which is illustrated in Figure 6.1.[5] Written back in 1976, the testament remains a standard way of reinforcing IKEA's culture within the organization. Consider those points in the testament that tie back to IKEA's emphasis on creativity and spontaneity:

*Profit gives us resources.* This places an explicit emphasis on using profits to feed creative renewal within the organization.

*Reaching good results with small means.* The easiest solutions to all kinds of problems are often the most expensive and mediocre. Creative solutions make improvements without wasting resources.

*Simplicity is a virtue.* The more complicated the organization and its solutions, the more paralysis or lack of creativity that results.

*Doing it a different way.* IKEA employees are encouraged to question why things are done in a certain way and are dared to be different.

*Taking responsibility is a privilege.* Employees are reminded to exercise their right and privilege to make decisions and take responsibility. The fear of making mistakes is the enemy of development and the root of bureaucracy.

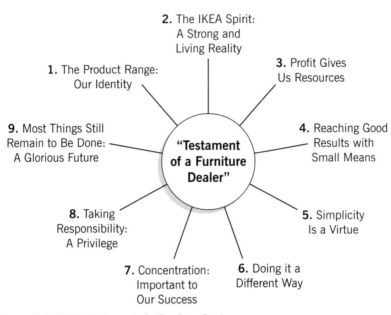

**2.** The IKEA Spirit: A Strong and Living Reality

**3.** Profit Gives Us Resources

**1.** The Product Range: Our Identity

**9.** Most Things Still Remain to Be Done: A Glorious Future

"Testament of a Furniture Dealer"

**4.** Reaching Good Results with Small Means

**8.** Taking Responsibility: A Privilege

**5.** Simplicity Is a Virtue

**7.** Concentration: Important to Our Success

**6.** Doing it a Different Way

**Figure 6.1.** IKEA's Testament of a Furniture Dealer

*Lead the way!* Of course, a service leader is far more than just another participant in this process. As the title of this chapter suggests, an organization looks to its leaders to generate ideas, make decisions, and lead the way. Good ideas have a way of getting lost in organizations. One of your primary jobs as a service leader is to keep track of not just your own ideas but also those generated by your employees and customers. In many cases your job boils down to being the number one advocate for someone else's idea! As Eisner says, "Sometimes all that good ideas or good people need is an advocate who won't shut up."[6] But even the ideas of others must fit into an overall service strategy that you set. It is up to the leaders in any organization to decide how much or how little to infuse technology into its offerings and where the organization should position itself on the goods-to-services continuum.

## ■ Are Your Activities Focused?

*Keep your activities focused!* Remaining disciplined and focused on your target customers shouldn't kill creativity. In fact, it takes tremendous creativity to innovate within constraints. As we have argued throughout, your linked activities or seamless system will rupture unless you retain a constancy of purpose. Don't just grow for the sake of growing. Good growth occurs when you add value for existing customers or replicate your linked activities for targeted customers not yet served.

*Understand the gestalt!* Discipline and focus require an understanding of your service organization as a whole. The business world is filled with attempts to oversimplify. You must avoid the temptation of adopting simplistic answers to complex questions. Improving customer satisfaction or increasing customer loyalty cannot be viewed as stand-alone solutions to your business problems. Service leaders understand their business model from a systems perspective. Profits provide resources, resources create a satisfied and committed workforce, your workforce co-produces a service offering with your customers, customers have a great experience, and these customers become your friends and partners.

Service leaders also understand how new ideas, concepts, and technologies fit into the big picture. Your linked activities are like an ecosystem that can be tapped or leveraged, but whose equilibrium must be maintained. For example, when IKEA was about to open its San Francisco store it used an e-mail campaign to enlist its customers to spread the word.[7] It offered savings of up to $75 if customers passed along an on-line "postcard" promoting the opening of the store to ten friends. Passing along the postcard to five friends netted the customer $25 off of a $150 purchase. IKEA initially ran into some trouble with the local media for encouraging "spamming," the sending of unsolicited ads through e-mail. To the company and its customers, however, the postcard process was just another example of how the IKEA model works. The cards included coupons to reward customers for their participation. And customers were in charge of choosing to whom they would send the cards. As one card recipient in the San Francisco area commented, "People are waiting for that place to open. I think there is a cult of IKEA going on . . . [the postcards] are just boosting the anticipation." Keeping the spamming issue in mind, the customer "tried to be careful; I didn't want to send it to anyone who would hate that sort of thing."[8] In the end, spamming was a nonissue. By understanding how its ecosystem worked, IKEA was able to enlist its customers to help it once again co-produce its offering. IKEA maintained the equilibrium in its ecosystem by reducing costs and delivering superior customer value.

### ■ A Final Word

Build the culture, link the activities, and stay focused! It's a deceptively simple concept that is difficult to implement. Service leaders must live the culture on a daily basis, be there for their employees, and keep the whole organization focused. Whether you are just beginning or are continuing your efforts to create a competitive service advantage, some soul searching is required. Your organization must understand its strengths, its weaknesses, and what it wants to be when it grows up. This may mean starting with the basics to improve things gone wrong, improving service performance and things gone right, or moving first to find innovative solutions to customer problems. The various cases and examples that we have used throughout the book, from the Ritz-Carlton and IKEA to Sterling Pulp Chemicals and SAS, illustrate how a wide variety of companies have managed the process.

We leave you with one last lesson of great service leaders. *Service leaders are temporary managers of great institutions!* If you see yourself as larger than the organization you manage, you're the wrong person for the job. Disney's Eisner views himself as a "temporary manager of a great institution."[9] IKEA's Kamprad focuses his efforts these days on IKEA's "eternal life." As long as the "many people" have a need for housing on earth, customers will have a need for a "strong and efficient IKEA."[10] Our world is oversupplied these days with managers who have been more worried about themselves than about ensuring the future of their institutions. From recent scandals involving Enron and Arthur Andersen, to K-Mart, to WorldCom, our trust in service organizations has been shaken.

We could all learn something from organizations and leaders who quietly and continually pursue goals that benefit everyone involved, from customers and investors to employees and society as a whole. Kamprad's concept of *good capitalism* is often lost in a world that fixates on growth, profits, and stock prices. He has long argued that "people who work for IKEA believe that they really are working for a better society and that they therefore like working for IKEA. They believe that in their daily lives they are contributing to a better world."[11] We hope that you have learned from this book how to better compete through services and to profit from your linked activities. But unless you use those profits to invest in your employees, customers, and communities, you'll find it impossible to keep a good thing going.

## CHAPTER SUMMARY

Our case studies and research provide important lessons regarding your role as a leader in a service economy. Great service leaders recognize that success depends on constantly building a culture, staying focused on customers, and linking activities in order to build a sustainable competitive advantage. To build and reinforce the culture, service leaders must live the company's values through direct interaction with both customers and employees. By focusing on employees, great service leaders recognize that it is their employees who provide customers with solutions and experiences. Great service leaders aren't content to focus on any one level of the service development hierarchy. Service leaders tap both customers and employees as sources of creativity within a constant process of removing things gone wrong, adding things gone right, and innovating.

Leadership requires saying no to those improvements or innovations that are inconsistent with a company's strategy. Remaining focused on target customers focuses one's creativity and keeps a seamless system of linked activities from bursting. Your linked activities are a type of ecosystem that can grow if some equilibrium is maintained. This requires understanding how new ideas, concepts, and technology fit into the big picture. Finally, service leaders don't let their own egos supplant the ecosystem that they manage. Great service leaders understand that they are but temporary managers of great institutions.

**Questions for Consideration**

Use the lessons discussed in the chapter to evaluate your own strengths and weaknesses as a service leader and to identify specific areas in which you could improve. Specifically, how well do you

1. Live the culture?
2. Manage by walking around?
3. Focus on employees?
4. Manage all levels of service development (remove things gone wrong, add things gone right, and innovate) simultaneously?
5. Emphasize creativity and spontaneity on a daily basis?
6. Lead the way by advocating what is consistent with your service strategy?
7. Remain focused on your target customers?
8. Understand the gestalt or ecosystem in which your company operates?
9. View yourself as a temporary manager of a great institution?

# Appendix:
# The IKEA Saga

T he following excerpt from an article "The IKEA Saga" is
reprinted with permission from the authors, Bo Edvardsson
and Bo Enquist, and the publisher.*

## ■ Act I: The Period When Ingvar Kamprad Created IKEA and Its Different Concepts

To open a Saga you have to start with history. The stone walls of
Småland (a poor county in the southern part of Sweden) symbolize the soul of IKEA. Ingvar Kamprad was born in that region, and it is here that IKEA's heart still remains. It was in this
region the IKEA Saga started.

*"Our Hearts Stay in Småland"*
IKEA has its roots in Småland, historically one of Sweden's
poorest regions, where the harsh countryside demands thrift,
inventiveness and hard work. Many small businesses,

*Bo Edvardsson and Bo Enquist, "The IKEA Saga: How Service Culture Drives
Strategy," *Service Industries Journal* (2002, vol. 22, no. 4, pp. 153–186). We thank
the authors and the publisher for permitting us to reprint this piece.

craftsmen and traders are found here. It was here that Ingvar Kamprad was born in 1926 on a farm called Elmtaryd in the village of Agunnaryd, a few miles outside Älmhult, the heart of IKEA. Product development, quality control and catalogue production is still controlled from Älmhult. And it is here that IKEA has its central warehouse for Northern Europe.

When IKEA started to sell furniture at factory prices by mail order in the early 1950s, it met with firm resistance from the established furniture trade. Suppliers were threatened with boycotts and IKEA was literally thrown out of the bid furniture trade fair in Stockholm. But customers poured in. And the corporate spirit from Småland could not be broken. Problems were turned into opportunities. That's the story behind what forms the foundation of our operations today. With its own catalogue, its own stores, enthusiastic employees, suppliers all over the world, self-assembly furniture in flat packages, Möbelfakta and motivated customers who can save themselves money through their own efforts.

IKEA has found its own niche: beautiful, inexpensive and durable furniture for the majority of people. Not just in Sweden, but worldwide. We have met a need that nobody bothered about. And the response has been fantastic. But the way has sometimes been as stony and uneven as a field in Småland. And that's why stone walls, a monument to human perseverance and optimism, symbolize our corporate culture.

We have developed and refined our vision: To contribute to a better everyday life for the majority of people. We have grown at our own pace and through our own strengths. Learnt from our own and others' mistakes. Never sat back and relaxed.[1]

In Act I we want to retell three stories of how core IKEA concepts were born. It is about catalogue and store as one unit; the first Self-Assemble Furniture and how Poland became the key for low cost production.

### The Concepts Catalogue and Store as One Unit

The first story is about how Ingvar Kamprad and Sven Göte Hansson, the first employee in IKEA, in 1951 created a joint venture between a mail order firm and a store:

> Sven Göte came into my life at a time when Ikéa (the first trademark) was very much at a crossroad. Competition in mail order had become almost unendurable. . . . Step by step, this price war affected the quality. . . . We were faced with a momentous decision: to allow Ikéa to die or to find a new way of maintaining the trust of the customer and still make money. Out of long talks through the night with Sven Göte about how we were to get out of this vicious circle—lower price, worse quality—the idea grew of trying a permanent display or exhibition of our furniture. People could go to the display, see the furniture for themselves, and compare the quality at different price levels.

The solution became a shabby building in Älmhult (Albin Lagerblad's joinery) for the enormous sum of 13,000 kronor ($1,625 compared with a modern store over 30 million dollars). Ingvar Kamprad continues:

> In the autumn of 1952, we completed the catalogue, which came out in time for opening of the furniture exhibition on March 18, 1953. . . . We displayed our furniture on two levels. We could now at last show those cheap ironing boards alongside those that cost five kronor more and were of good quality. And people did just what we had hoped: they wisely chose the more expensive ironing board. At that moment, the basis of the modern IKEA concept was created, and in principle it still applies: first and foremost, use a catalogue to tempt people to come to an exhibition, which today is our store.[2]

## The Story of the First Self-Assemble Furniture

IKEA is well known for its "Self-Assemble" Furniture concept. Kamprad tells how the whole idea started. He talks about himself and Gillis Lundgren who was at that time a young draftsman at an advertising agency:

> That was the beginning of our designing our own furniture, essentially avoiding the boycott and its problems. But on one occasion when we had photographed a table and were to pack it up again afterward, it was Gillis who muttered something like "God, what a lot of space it takes up. Let's take the legs off and put them under the tabletop." That one fine day—or was it a night?—we had our first flat parcel, and thus we started a revolution. In the 1953 catalogue, which was ready in 1952, "Max," the very first self-assemble table, was included. After that followed a whole series of other self-assemble furniture, and by 1956 the concept was more or less systematized.[3]

## Poland: The Key to Low Cost Production

Another very important event in IKEA was its need for more production capacity. Because of the boycott from the established furniture dealers to those furniture manufacturers who were supplying IKEA, in combination with a sales success of some of its furniture, IKEA had to find more production capacity outside Sweden. That was in the early 60s and here is the story of how Poland, at that time a communist country, became the solution. Kamprad and his newly appointed colleague for purchasing furniture, engineer Ragnar Sterte, looked for new capacity. On January 21, 1961, Kamprad, his father, and Ragnar Sterte landed in Warsaw. Their visit lasted a week.[4] Here comes Ingvar Kamprad's story:

> When we saw the first wretched photographs of their products and the prices they offered us at the PAGED office, and when it became evident that we couldn't even leave Warsaw to go and

see the manufactures, I announced our definite lack of interest. We were close to packing our bags and going home.[5]

The crisis was solved, but it took a long time before consumer quality standards (quality assurance) took root in Poland. Kamprad continues:

> At first we did a bit of advance smuggling. Illegally, we took tools such as files, spare parts for machines, and even carbon for ancient typewriters. . . . We bought nose and mouth protectors when we saw the dreadful environment, and we took a whole lot of second-hand machines from a firm in Jönköping and installed them in Poland instead. . . . Slowly and with repeated reverses, we helped to build up a modern furniture industry.[6]

The end of this story will be very important for the future. Poland is today the natural bridgehead to the new potential market in Russia.

### ■ Act II: The Search for Eternal Life for IKEA

Act II tells stories about the enormous expanding internationalization period and also later at the same time a consolidation period. Here we draw upon parts of "holy documents" from the founder as well as narratives of important events in IKEA's history such as a new president for IKEA and the problems IKEA has had in North America.

#### Creating the Inaccessible Company

Ingvar Kamprad had decided to leave Sweden and go abroad. It was in the early 1970s. He says:

> I asked myself, for several reasons: What do we do now? How can we keep the future IKEA without inheritance taxes

bleeding the company to death or family squabbles between sons ruining it? How can we avoid greedy interests endangering what we have built up, while keeping a dynamic and creative organization? And how can moves abroad be achieved without personally affecting my family and me in a financially devastating way?

Torekull explains Ingvar Kamprad's idea of "eternal life" for IKEA.

When Ingvar Kamprad decided to go abroad, his ambition was undeniable to give his lifework the best possible chance of "eternal life." Long after he passed away, he wanted the company to be able to develop and flourish. In his own words, "As long as there is human housing on our earth, there will be a need for a strong and efficient IKEA." But his ambition went further than that. No one and nothing was to destroy or endanger his business vision, whether a member of the family or market forces or politicians. Barriers were to be constructed against not only hostile assaults but also against the danger that belies apathy. All the dynamism was to be guaranteed as long as it was humanly possible. More than that, IKEA was a concept to be protected in the event of war and subversive political changes. And power—that was ultimately to lead back to the family in the future as well.[7]

The solution was that IKEA is governed by a double command structure. Torekull talks about "the spirit" which takes care of the concept and "the hand" which takes care of the operation. Inter IKEA Systems B.V. (a holding company in Luxembourg) is the owner and franchiser of the IKEA concept and has a coordination office in Belgium outside Brussels. IKEA retailers worldwide operate on a franchise basis. Most IKEA retailers belong to the IKEA Group (the hand). The IKEA Group includes most IKEA retailers, the product development center IKEA of Sweden

AB and IKEA trading and wholesaling companies. The IKEA Group is owned by the double Dutch foundation, the Stichting INGKA Foundation/Stichting IKEA Foundation and has all shares in INGKA Holding B.V., the group of companies that consists of IKEA (all the stores and factories and offices). The IKEA Group activities are coordinated by IKEA International A/S in Denmark situated in Humlebeack outside Copenhagen.[8]

There is also a third group IKANO that is controlled 100% by the Kamprad family. In this group there are businesses that sometimes have relations to IKEA and sometimes not as Financial Services, Banking, Real Estate Investment, Insurance and 100 Habitat Stores.

### The Testament of a Furniture Dealer

The strong culture in IKEA can give IKEA an image to be a religion. In this aspect the testament will be a holy script and it is about "to create a better everyday life for the majority of people." We can from the preface written by Ingvar Kamprad read the following:

Once and for all we have decided to side with the many. What is good for our customers is also good for us in the long run. This is an objective that entails responsibility.

In all countries and social systems, eastern as well as western, a disproportionately large part of all resources is used to satisfy a small part of the population. In our line of business for instance, too many new and beautifully designed products can be afforded by only a small group of better-off people. IKEA's aim is to change this situation.

Already after little more than two decades of operation we believe we have had some success. A well-known industrialist/politician once said that IKEA has had a greater impact on the democratization process than many political measures combined. We also think that our activities have inspired many of our competitors to work in the same direction. During the past two decades, IKEA has changed the face of the furniture industry in Sweden and, increasingly, throughout the world. Our revolutionary methods of design, manufacture, and distribution have made fine furniture available and affordable for the majority of people—for all those with limited budgets. . . .

After this preface the testament is divided in nine points as follows: (1) The Product Range—our Identity, (2) The IKEA Spirit: A Strong and Living Reality, (3) Profit Gives us Resources, (4) To Reach Good Results with Small Means, (5) Simplicity Is A Virtue, (6) The Different Way, (7) Concentration of Energy— Important to Our Success, (8) To Assume Responsibility—A Privilege, (9) Most Things Still Remain To Be Done. A Glorious Future!

In February 1996 Ingvar Kamprad came once again with a reprint of his testament but this time complemented with special *words* as an important part of the IKEA heritage. These words are: *humbleness; will-power; simplicity; the majority of people; making do; experience; think differently; never say never; fear of making mistakes; status; . . . the IKEA way; bureaucracy; honesty; common sense; cost-consciousness; accepting and delegating responsibility; facing up to reality; solidarity and enthusiasm.* One of these words is important to look deeper into because it is connected to the IKEA vision. That's about "the majority of people." Here Kamprad writes the following:

*The Majority of People*
We have decided to stand on the side of the majority of people, which involves taking on more responsibility than might at first seem to be the case. Standing on the side of the majority of people means representing the interests of ordinary people, no matter whether that is good or bad for our own, short-term interests. It means getting rid of designs which are difficult and expensive to produce, even if they are easy to sell. It means re-

fusing to sell in hard currency to consumers in countries with non-convertible currencies, even though that would make our profits bigger and our problems fewer. Developing a range and presenting it in an imaginative, appealing way in all our stores demands a great deal of knowledge about the lives, hopes and aspirations of the majority of people. The best way to learn this is through personal experience, not as tourists gaping at things with our camera slung round our necks. Using public transport is one good example of how to get nearer to people. . . .[9]

Another word that is very important for the "believers" in IKEA is "the IKEA way." The word can be constructive but it can also be an excuse to remain as it is.

*The IKEA Way*
Our most misused expression. If you don't have any other comment to make, you can always make the excuse that this isn't really "the IKEA way" of doing things. What we really mean when we talk about "the IKEA way of doing things" is the sum of all of our values, the amalgamation of everything we believe in.[10]

The IKEA way is also a management program in IKEA, a program to reproduce and develop the strong IKEA culture. Mirriam Salzer explains this in her book about IKEA:

Today IKEA Way seminars are held a couple of times each year, as a week-long seminar in Älmhult. Managers from all IKEA units will meet Ingvar Kamprad, the founder of the Group, who on the first evening talks about IKEA's philosophy. During the following days the participants are given lectures on IKEA's history, the product range, the distribution system, the human resource idea etc. On the last day, there is a small ceremony at which the participants receive a pin which is a miniature IKEA insert key. This is a token of having become an "IKEA ambassador," a "culture-bearer" with "a license" to

☐

spread the IKEA culture at "Mini-IKEA Way" seminars in his or her own organization.[11]

## A New President for IKEA

Anders Moberg became Ingvar Kamprad's successor in 1986. He is the second generation leader in IKEA and he has his roots in Småland. He gives his version of his vision how to develop IKEA for the next decades.

> We are changing things in practically all of the twenty-five major stores. . . . Twenty of these major stores, all situated in capital cities, make up over 35 percent of IKEA's sales, and account for over 60 percent of profit; developing them is the basis for being able to realize other projects. These stores, some selling over one billion kronor, must have more parking space, more toilets, more bank machines, and a greater capacity for everything that makes shopping more tolerable for customers and keeps the wear and tear in check.[12]

The strategy for IKEA is to penetrate every market more deeply. Moberg continues:

> In the United States (where things are going better and better), an expensive marketing strategy demands a higher marketing cover. But elsewhere as well, the rule is, the deeper the penetration, the better the cost structure, the more IKEA can invest in the volume that is its trump card in competition.[13]

## Cost-Consciousness

Cost-consciousness is one of these "words" which is sacred in IKEA. Here we can hear the official version of this "virtue."

> This notion is probably the easiest to understand, because it goes hand in hand with our business idea. Our low prices are

written into our business idea as an essential condition for our success. Anyone can tell you that it is impossible to have a low price, good quality and good profitability if you don't have low costs. So cost-consciousness has to permeate everything we do, almost to the point of that kind of exaggerated meanness that others may call "penny-pinching."[14]

It is also notable that IKEA is looking very close at its cash-flow and therefore they don't want to be drained by what they call "non creative costs," which for IKEA means taxes. Anders Moberg says about this cost: "The IKEA business view of taxation is simple and straightforward. We follow all the laws and regulation, but if the laws give certain relief, we exploit these opportunities."[15]

### "The America Lesson"

North America is not like Europe. This is a lesson which has taken more than 20 years for IKEA to learn and to go from being in the "red" to the "black" when it comes to business results. But when you have learnt, as IKEA has done, the potential is enormous. Anders Moberg once said: "Nothing contradicts the possibility that IKEA North America will one day produce sales and make a profit as big as today's total IKEA sales in all the world combined."[16]

But it has taken a long time for IKEA to come to that position. North America is not a Kamprad project. Instead he used to say: "The next generation will have to take care of North America."[17] This was what his successor, president Anders Moberg, did.

Let us see the American lesson on a narrative level. Nordin, in charge of the U.S. market product range, tells the story for Bertil Torekull, and he retold the story in the following way:

> He will never forget an occasion in the new Houston store when he suddenly got one bright idea. A woman had stopped

in front of a double bed with a look of admiration and puzzle-
ment when Nordin offered his help. Yes, the lady was crazy
about the bed, but what in the world did "160 cm" mean?
Nordin remembers delving into a complicated lecture on
buying facts and the metric system, explaining that this was
an accepted measurement of a double bed in Sweden. The
woman looked at him quizzically and said: "Young man, I
have no clue what you are talking about. You really have no
king-size or queen-size beds?" and walked out. This was the
eye-opener for Nordin.[18]

After this a lot changed. Torekull put it this way: "Slowly
but surely, the staffs in both Älmhult and IKEA North America
have begun to understand the potential benefits of working together. The clash of cultures, not seen in the beginning, is now
examined in detail, and the resulting decisions affect IKEA in
both directions across the Atlantic." Nordin is today sales direc-
tor for North America. He says about the IKEA operation in
North America: "No stock exchange company would ever have
accepted the weak development we reported in the beginning.
But since long-range timing and patience is an IKEA credo, we
had time to rethink and build a partly new base for survival."[19]

It has taken three leaders for IKEA North America for the
operation to generate profits. Torekull gives his comments on
these three leaders.

> You can say that the first boss of IKEA North America, Björn
> Bayley, laid down a foundation of down-to-earth wisdom
> and loyalty on which the more visionary thinking of Göran
> Carstedt—who built six new stores and prepared the mega-
> store in Chicago—could skillfully be based. Now Jan Kjellman,
> the latest in charge, following a tough financial and structural
> reorganization, can purposefully harvest the fruits from two
> decades of struggle and sometimes bitter lessons. His mission
> is to increase market share and improve profits at the speed of
> two new North American stores per year.[20]

IKEA is now on the right track in the U.S. We can hear the story when this also became true in "the books."

Therefore, on an early January morning in 1999, you hear the smattering of applause in the employee cafeteria of IKEA's headquarters in Philadelphia when the young accountant Jill Matherson presents the results from the first quarter. For the first time, costs have dropped below the magic mark of 30 percent of sales; the cost increase is a smaller percentage of sales than the preliminary profit; the new Chicago store has reached the break-even point after only forty-five days; and Elizabeth (New York, one of the "major" stores) is increasing its profit by 43 percent in record fashion.[21]

### "Good Capitalism" and Trade with Responsibility

IKEA is not like a traditional globalized company. Below we can listen to two stories about how Kamprad looks at capitalism and later Moberg looks at global trade. Those stories have a very important impact on how IKEA acts as a company with social consciousness. Ingvar Kamprad and his view of capitalism is "the dream of the good capitalism." He says:

Can capitalism be good? In what way can I as an entrepreneur be of the most use? How is an empathetic businessman to orient himself between a centrally governed society with in-built economic and social support for its citizens and a market economy that only too easily bolts at top speed at the expense of individuals? I admit that I have thought a great deal about these matters. . . . The question is whether, as an entrepreneur, I can combine the good in a profit-making business with a lasting human social vision. I like to think it must be possible. I don't mean to say that capitalism can avoid fiascos. I myself have been the cause of several. To fail is part of all evolution. But every day, IKEA strives to develop and achieve a better future for the people, our customers. A company goal of that kind influences those working toward it. Studies show that people who work for IKEA believe that they really are working for a better society and that they therefore like working for IKEA. They believe that in their daily lives they are contributing to a better world.[22]

The social and democratic side of the above discussion from Ingvar Kamprad is about responsibility. Anders Moberg has been a spokesman for this in IKEA for the future. In a debate article in one of the leading newspapers in Sweden in 1997 he said that "trade is better than aid." In a 1999 IKEA Magazine (Issue number 1) for its employees we can read about "trade with responsibility" and that IKEA cooperates with other companies in a network led by the Institute of Social and Ethical Accountability—ISEA. The network's task is to develop working models in social accountability on much the same lines as those that already exist for quality and environmental work. Anders Moberg explains the IKEA standpoint in the same magazine.

Today IKEA buys products from over 2,300 suppliers in 64 countries. One third of all we purchase comes from Asia and Eastern Europe, the rest from the west. We are increasing our purchases in Asia, but this region is often singled out by the media for poor working conditions. Admittedly, the situation in many factories is unacceptable from a western point of view. We are working together with our suppliers on development programs that address working conditions, child labor issues and environmental questions. . . . But I'm convinced that cross-border cooperation leads to development. Hundreds of thousands of workers in our suppliers' factories depend on the fact that IKEA assumes a responsible attitude to its long-term commitments. We create employment, we open markets for these people's products—and we work together with our suppliers to make constant improvements. IKEA is a commercial company, but there is a social side to our vision and our business idea. Only by being open and honest can we create the right conditions to keep improving everyday life for the many people.[23]

### Epilogue of Act II

In the spring of 1999 we can read a press release from IKEA that:

> The Board has appointed Anders Dahlvig as new President of the IKEA Group, and he will together with Hans Gydell lead IKEA into the future. Anders Moberg has, after almost thirty years within IKEA, out of which almost half the time as its President, decided to accept new challenges outside the company. (Anders Moberg's new employer is the American company Home Depot and he will join the company as its first President-International).[24]

### ■ Act III: A New IKEA Generation Takes Over

The comments from Ingvar Kamprad about this change to "all in the worldwide IKEA family" are:

> Anders Dahlvig and Hans Gydell will lead us into the future. A great team with Anders Dahlvig as our new President, and Hans Gydell as his close liaison with an extended area of responsibility. I feel great happiness that both of them have accepted the new challenge, and, thus, we will be able to build on our leadership philosophy to realize our strategic decisions as IKEA is expanding. I have cooperated very closely with both Anders and Hans during many years; they are both enthusiastic carriers of our messages, which they have been part of creating. When I asked Anders Moberg about his successor we share the same opinion. I hope that you will feel the same joy of the new generation as my family and I do. . . .
>
> On behalf of the Board and my family, yours sincerely,
> Ingvar Kamprad, Älmhult, March 22, 1998

Anders Moberg also has a message to his colleagues world-wide:

> After having had the opportunity to grow and develop with IKEA for almost 30 years, out of which almost half the time as its President, I have decided to accept new challenges outside IKEA. To lead a company like IKEA has been extremely stimulating and meant continuous development and new challenges. I have worked together with fantastic colleagues, who have shown incredible support and loyalty. I have also had the privilege to work closely with and have as my mentor Ingvar Kamprad, one of the greatest entrepreneurs of our time, and this has of course meant a lot for my own development. I hope that Ingvar, and all of you, who have supported and helped me during the years, will not be too disappointed for my leaving you. Naturally, it feels very hard to say goodbye to all of you. Simultaneously, it feels good to leave at a time when IKEA is on the top and most things are going our way. Now I am leaving for new adventures in the world before I'm too old. . . .
>
> Anders Moberg, Humlebaeck, March 22, 1999

There are at this time very few new stories to tell the audience in act III. Will it be more of the same or will we see some changes? What we have heard so far is that it is "more of the same." The expansion in the U.S., the second largest market after Germany, will continue, and IKEA opened its first store in Russia in 2000.[25] We can also read that the IKEA-kitchen VÄRDE (Swedish word for value; all products in IKEA have a Swedish name) has been awarded the "Red Dot for Highest Design Quality" in Germany (IKEA Internet).

The IKEA Saga is not over. The new generation has taken over and will tell new stories as long as they are official IKEA ambassadors. Moberg is not an IKEA-man from Småland any longer, but the founder Ingvar Kamprad still has his address in Älmhult and will still be part of the Saga.

# Notes

**Chapter One**

1. Survey of Current Business [http://www.bea.doc.gov/bea/pubs.html]. (September 2001).
2. Bo Edvardsson and Anders Gustafsson, *The Nordic School of Quality Management* (Lund, Sweden: Studentlitteratur, 1999).
3. Christian Grönroos, *Services Management and Marketing: Managing the Moments of Truth in Service Competition* (San Francisco: New Lexington Press, 1990). See also Grönroos, "Marketing Services: The Case of the Missing Product," in *The Nordic School of Quality Management,* edited by Bo Edvardsson and Anders Gustafsson, 226–251 (Lund, Sweden: Studentlitteratur, 1999).
4. Michael D. Johnson and others, "An Introduction to Quality, Satisfaction, and Retention—Implications for the Automotive Industry," in *Customer Retention in the Automotive Industry: Quality, Satisfaction and Loyalty,* edited by Michael D. Johnson and others, 1–17 (Wiesbaden, Germany: Gabler, 1997).
5. B. Joseph Pine and James H. Gilmore, "Welcome to the Experience Economy," *Harvard Business Review 76* (July–August 1998): 97–105.
6. Source: www.nwa.com/corpinfo/newsc/awards.shtml (September 2002).

□

7. Roger Hallowell, *SOTHEBYS.COM* (2000), Harvard Business School Case no. 9-800-387.
8. See Bo Edvardsson and others, *New Service Development and Innovation in the New Economy* (Lund, Sweden: Studentlitteratur, 2000). See also Jeremy Hope and Tony Hope, *Competing in the Third Wave: The Ten Management Issues of the Information Age* (Boston: Harvard Business School Press, 1997).
9. C. K. Prahalad and Venkatram Ramaswamy, "Co-opting Customer Competence," *Harvard Business Review 78* (January-February 2000): 79–87.
10. See Michael D. Johnson and Anders Gustafsson, *Improving Customer Satisfaction, Loyalty, and Profit: An Integrated Measurement and Management System* (San Francisco: Jossey-Bass, 2000).
11. Claes Fornell and others, "The American Customer Satisfaction Index: Nature, Purpose and Findings," *Journal of Marketing* 60 (October 1996): 7–18.
12. Source: www.bus.umich.edu/research/nqrc/acsi.html (January 2003).

**Chapter Two**

1. Adapted from Aaron Brown and others, "Oracle 8i Appliance: Da Bomb or a Bomb?" (Ann Arbor: Multidisciplinary Action Project, University of Michigan Business School, 2000).
2. John E. Ettlie and Michael D. Johnson, "Product Development Benchmarking Versus Customer Focus in Applications of Quality Function Deployment," *Marketing Letters* 5, no. 2 (1994): 107–116.
3. Michael D. Johnson, *Customer Orientation and Market Action* (Upper Saddle River, N.J.: Prentice Hall, 1998).
4. Bo Edvardsson and others, *New Service Development and Innovation in the New Economy* (Lund, Sweden: Studentlitteratur, 2000).
5. Leonard L. Berry, *The Soul of Service: The Nine Drivers of Sustainable Business Success* (New York: Free Press, 1999).
6. James L. Heskett and others, "Putting the Service-Profit Chain to Work," *Harvard Business Review 72* (March–April 1994): 164–174.
7. M. Sheridan, "J. W. Marriott, Jr., Chairman and President, Marriott Corporation," *Sky Magazine* (March 1987): 46–53.

8. Benjamin Schneider and David E. Bowen, *Winning the Service Game* (Boston: Harvard Business School Press, 1995).

9. Source: www.bus.umich.edu/research/nqrc/acsi.html (January 2003).

10. Michael Treacy and Fried Wiersema, *The Discipline of Market Leaders: Choose Your Customers, Narrow Your Focus, Dominate Your Market* (Reading, Mass.: Perseus, 1997).

11. Roger J. Best, *Market-Based Management: Strategies for Growing Customer Value and Profitability,* 2nd ed. (Upper Saddle River, N.J.: Prentice Hall, 2000).

12. Adapted from Johnson, *Customer Orientation and Market Action.*

13. Adapted from Edvardsson and others, *New Service Development and Innovation in the New Economy.* See also Michael E. Porter, "What Is Strategy?" *Harvard Business Review 74* (November-December 1996): 61–78.

14. Adapted from Bo Edvardsson and Bo Enquist, "The IKEA Saga: How Service Culture Drives Strategy," *Service Industries Journal* 22, no. 4 (2002): 153–186.

15. From Anders Moberg and Ingvar Kamprad, "Our History," in *Meet IKEA: The Idea, the Company, the People,* internal document from InterIKEA Systems B.V., 42. Also available in Bertil Torekull, *Leading by Design: The IKEA Story* (New York: HarperBusiness, 1999).

16. Bertil Torekull, *Leading by Design: The IKEA Story* (New York: Harper-Business, 1999), 25.

17. From Torekull, *Leading by Design*, 52.

18. Torekull, *Leading by Design,* 60.

19. From Ingvar Kamprad, *A Little Dictionary*, internal document from InterIKEA Systems B.V., 21. Also available in Torekull, *Leading by Design.*

20. Suzy Wetlaufer, "Common Sense and Conflict: An Interview with Disney's Michael Eisner," *Harvard Business Review 78* (January–February 2000): 114–124.

21. Richard Wise and Peter Baumgartner, "Go Downstream: The New Profit Imperative in Manufacturing," *Harvard Business Review 77* (September–October 1999): 133–141.

22. Greg Brenneman, "Right Away and All at Once: How We Saved Continental," *Harvard Business Review 76* (September–October 1998): 2–12.

## Chapter Three

1. Lars Nilsson and Michael D. Johnson, "The Importance of Reliability and Customization from Goods to Services," *Quality Management Journal 10*, no. 1 (2003): 8–19.
2. Estimate based on multiple research studies from the Service Research Center, Karlstad University, Sweden (see www.ctf.kau.se).
3. W. Edwards Deming, *Quality, Productivity and Competitive Position* (Cambridge, Mass.: MIT Press, 1982).
4. From personal interview with Suzanne Boda, vice president, customer service, Northwest Airlines (May 2002).
5. Alan F. Dutka, *AMA Handbook for Customer Satisfaction* (Chicago: American Marketing Association, 1994).
6. Christopher W. L. Hart, "The Power of Unconditional Service Guarantees," *Harvard Business Review* (July-August 1998): 54–61.
7. Amy Smith, Ruth Bolton, and Janet Wagner, "A Model of Customer Satisfaction with Service Encounters Involving Failure and Recovery," *Journal of Marketing Research,* 36 (August 1999): 356–372.
8. Richard A. Krueger, *Focus Groups: A Practical Guide for Applied Research* (Thousand Oaks, Calif.: Sage, 1988).
9. Abbie Griffin and John R. Hauser, "The Voice of the Customer," *Marketing Science* 12 (Winter 1993): 1–27.
10. Griffin and Hauser, "The Voice of the Customer."
11. Bob E. Hayes, *Measuring Customer Satisfaction: Survey Design, Use, and Statistical Analysis Methods* (Milwaukee, Wis.: ASQ Quality Press, 1998).
12. Bernd Stauss and B. Weinlich, "Process-Oriented Measurement of Service Quality: Applying the Sequential Incident Method," *European Journal of Marketing* 31, no. 1 (1997): 33–55.
13. Inger Roos, "Switching Processes in Customer Relationships," *Journal of Service Research* 2 (August 1999): 68–85.
14. Leonard L. Berry, *On Great Service: A Framework for Action* (New York: Free Press, 1995).
15. Adapted from Berry, *On Great Service.*
16. See Masaaki Imai, *Gemba Kaizen: A Commonsense, Low-Cost Approach to Management* (New York: McGraw-Hill, 1997).

17. Source: Ritz-Carlton Hotels, internal communication.
18. Peter S. Pande, Robert P. Neuman, and Roland R. Cavanagh, *The Six Sigma Way: How GE, Motorola, and Other Top Companies Are Honing Their Performance* (New York: McGraw-Hill, 2000).
19. Source: Ritz-Carlton Hotels, internal communication.

**Chapter Four**

1. Bo Edvardsson and others, *New Service Development and Innovation in the New Economy* (Lund, Sweden: Studentlitteratur, 2000).
2. Michael D. Johnson and Anders Gustafsson, *Improving Customer Satisfaction, Loyalty and Profit: An Integrated Measurement and Management System* (San Francisco: Jossey-Bass, 2000).
3. A. Parasuraman, Leonard L. Berry, and Valarie A. Zeithaml, "Refinement and Reassessment of the SERVQUAL Scale," *Journal of Retailing* 67, no. 4 (1991): 420–450.
4. Johnson and Gustafsson, *Improving Customer Satisfaction, Loyalty and Profit.*
5. John A. Martilla and John C. James, "Importance-Performance Analysis," *Journal of Marketing* 41 (Winter 1977): 77–79. See also Michael D. Johnson, *Customer Orientation and Market Action* (Upper Saddle River, N.J.: Prentice Hall, 1998).
6. C. J. Easingwood, "New Product Development for Service Companies," *Journal of Product Innovation Management* 3 (December 1986): 264–275.
7. D. Teixeira and J. Ziskin, "Achieving Quality with Customers in Mind," *Bankers Magazine* (January-February 1993): 29–35.
8. Michael E. Porter, "What Is Strategy?" *Harvard Business Review 74* (November-December 1996): 61–78.
9. Leonard L. Berry, *The Soul of Service: The Nine Drivers of Sustainable Business Success* (New York: Free Press, 1999).
10. Berry, *The Soul of Service.*
11. Bo Edvardsson, "Quality in New Service Development: Key Concepts and a Frame of Reference," *International Journal of Production Economics* 52 (1997): 31–46.

12. S. S. Tax and I. Stuart, "Designing and Implementing New Services: The Challenges of Integrating Service Systems," *Journal of Retailing* 73, no. 1 (1997): 105–134.

13. This example and discussion draws upon Mark Nakashima, LeHardrix Plummer, and Suling Yan, "The Best Buy Customer Service Evolution," course paper (Ann Arbor: University of Michigan Business School, 2002).

14. Laurette Dubé, Michael D. Johnson, and Leo Mark Renaghan, "Adapting the QFD Approach to Extended Service Transactions," *Production and Operations Management* 8, no. 3 (1999): 301–317.

15. Dubé, Johnson, and Renaghan, "Adapting the QFD Approach to Extended Service Transactions." See also Glen Mazur, "Service QFD: State of the Art," in *Proceedings of the Third Annual International QFD Symposium: Vol. 1,* 57–66, edited by A. Gustafsson, B. Bergman, and F. Ekdahl (Linköping, Sweden: Linköping University, 1997).

16. From Anders Gustafsson and Michael D. Johnson, "Bridging the Quality-Satisfaction Gap," *Quality Management Journal 4,* no. 3 (1997): 27–43.

17. Adapted from Sally Sadosky, "Customer Satisfaction at IKEA," course paper (Ann Arbor: University of Michigan Business School, 1996).

18. Reprinted with the permission of InterIKEA Services B.V.

**Chapter Five**

1. Michael L. Tushman and Charles A. O'Reilly III, *Winning Through Innovation,* 2nd ed. (Boston: Harvard Business School Press, 2002).

2. Joe Tidd, John Bessant, and Keith Pavitt, *Managing Innovation: Integrating Technological, Market and Organizational Change,* 2nd ed. (New York: Wiley, 2001).

3. C. Merle Crawford, "Marketing Research and the New Product Failure Rate," *Journal of Marketing* (April 1977): 51–61. Glen L. Urban, John R. Hauser, and D. Nikhilesh, *Essentials of New Product Management* (Upper Saddle River, N.J.: Prentice Hall, 1987). R. G. Cooper, *Winning at New Products—Accelerating the Process from Idea to Launch,* 2nd ed. (Reading, Mass.: Addison-Wesley, 1993).

4. Valarie A. Zeithaml and Mary Jo Bitner, *Services Marketing: Integrating Customer Focus Across the Firm,* international 2nd ed. (Boston: Irwin McGraw-Hill, 2000).
5. Richard Normann, *Service Management* (Malmö, Sweden: Liber, 2000).
6. A. Parasuraman, "Technology Readiness Index (TRI): A Multiple-Item Scale to Measure Readiness to Embrace New Technologies," *Journal of Service Research* 2, no. 4 (2000): 307–320.
7. Quoted in Jeffrey E. Garten, *The Mind of the CEO* (Reading, Mass.: Perseus, 2001), 137.
8. For a complete description of these methods, see Michael D. Johnson, *Customer Orientation and Market Action* (Upper Saddle River, N.J.: Prentice Hall, 1998).
9. Tidd, Bessant, and Pavitt, *Managing Innovation.*
10. Geert Hofstede, *Culture's Consequences: Comparing Values, Behaviors, Institutions, and Organizations Across Nations,* 2nd ed. (Thousand Oaks, Calif.: Sage, 2001).
11. John E. Ettlie, *Managing Technological Innovation* (New York: Wiley, 2000).
12. See, for example, Eric A. von Hippel, *The Sources of Innovation* (Oxford: Oxford University Press, 1988).
13. Tushman and O'Reilly III, *Winning Through Innovation,* 35.
14. Quoted in Garten, *The Mind of the CEO,* 136.
15. C. K. Prahalad and Venkatram Ramaswamy, "Co-opting Customer Competence," *Harvard Business Review 78* (January-February 2000): 79–87.
16. Parts of this case are adapted from Bo Edvardsson and others, *New Service Development and Innovation in the New Economy* (Lund, Sweden: Studentlitteratur, 2000).
17. The research described in this case was conducted in cooperation with the Doblin Group. See www.doblin.com/who/index.html.
18. Per Kristensson, Peter R. Magnusson, and Jonas Matthing, "Users as a Hidden Resource for Creativity: Findings from an Experimental Study on User Involvement," *Creativity and Innovation Management* 11, no. 1 (2002): 55–61. See also Per Kristensson, Anders Gustafsson, and

□

Trevor Archer, "Harnessing the Creative Potential Among Users," working paper (Karlstad, Sweden: Service Research Center, 2002).
19. See von Hippel, *The Sources of Innovation.*

### Chapter Six

1. Quoted in Suzy Wetlaufer, "Common Sense and Conflict: An Interview with Disney's Michael Eisner," *Harvard Business Review 78* (January-February 2000): 114–124.
2. Leonard L. Berry and A. Parasuraman, *Marketing Services: Competing Through Quality* (New York: Free Press, 1991).
3. Leonard L. Berry, *The Soul of Service: The Nine Drivers of Sustainable Business Success* (New York: Free Press, 1999).
4. Quoted in Wetlaufer, "Common Sense and Conflict," 116.
5. Source: *Testament,* an internal presentation by InterIKEA Systems B.V. (2002).
6. Quoted in Wetlaufer, "Common Sense and Conflict," 122.
7. Stefanie Olsen, "IKEA Enlists Friends for Email Publicity," CNET News.com. http://news.cnet.com/news/0-1007-200-1567728.html?tag=prntfr (2000).
8. Olsen, "IKEA Enlists Friends for Email Publicity."
9. Quoted in Wetlaufer, "Common Sense and Conflict," 123.
10. Ingvar Kamprad, *A Little Dictionary,* internal document from Inter-IKEA Systems B.V., 28.
11. Bo Edvardsson and Bo Enquist, "The IKEA Saga: How Service Culture Drives Strategy," *Service Industries Journal* 22, no. 4 (2002): 153–186.

### Appendix

1. From Anders Moberg and Ingvar Kamprad, *Meet IKEA: The Idea, the Company, the People,* internal document from InterIKEA Systems B.V., 42. Also available in Bertil Torekull, *Leading by Design: The IKEA Story* (New York: HarperBusiness, 1999).
2. Bertil Torekull, *Leading by Design: The IKEA Story* (New York: HarperBusiness, 1999), 25.

3. Quoted in Torekull, *Leading by Design,* 52.
4. Torekull, *Leading by Design,* 58.
5. Quoted in Torekull, *Leading by Design,* 59.
6. Quoted in Torekull, *Leading by Design,* 60.
7. Torekull, *Leading by Design,* 97.
8. Torekull, *Leading by Design,* 100–103. "IKEA Facts and Figures," available at www.ikea.com/about_ikea/about.asp (2002).
9. From Ingvar Kamprad, *A Little Dictionary,* internal document from InterIKEA Systems B.V., 21. Also available in Bertil Torekull, *Leading by Design: The IKEA Story* (New York: HarperBusiness, 1999).
10. Kamprad, *A Little Dictionary,* 28.
11. M. Salzer, *Identity Across Borders: A Study in the "IKEA-World,"* doctoral dissertation (Linköping, Sweden: Department of Management and Economics, Linköping University, 1994), 145.
12. Torekull, *Leading by Design,* 188.
13. Torekull, *Leading by Design,* 189.
14. Kamprad, *A Little Dictionary,* 28.
15. Quoted in Torekull, *Leading by Design,* 185.
16. Quoted in Torekull, *Leading by Design,* 199.
17. Quoted in Torekull, *Leading by Design,* 192.
18. Quoted in Torekull, *Leading by Design,* 196.
19. Quoted in Torekull, *Leading by Design,* 195.
20. Torekull, *Leading by Design,* 198–199.
21. Torekull, *Leading by Design,* 199.
22. Torekull, *Leading by Design,* 153.
23. Anders Moberg, "Trade with Responsibility," *IKEA Info Magazine,* no. 1 (1999): 10–11.
24. "A New IKEA Generation Takes Over," press release (Humlebaek, Denmark, March 22, 1999).
25. "A New IKEA Generation Takes Over."

# The Authors

Anders Gustafsson is associate professor of business economics in the Service Research Center at Karlstad University, Sweden. He holds a Master of Science in industrial engineering and management and a Licentiate degree, Ph.D., and docent title, all in the subject of quality management, from Linköping University. Gustafsson teaches a variety of courses at universities in Sweden and in executive education programs nationally and internationally (Europe and Asia). He has also carried out a variety of national and international consulting projects for companies such as Ericsson, Volvo, and Daimler-Chrysler.

Gustafsson is author or coauthor of six other books: *Improving Customer Satisfaction, Loyalty, and Profit: An Integrated Measurement and Management System* (Jossey-Bass, 2000), *New Service Development and Innovation in the New Economy* (Studentlitteratur, 2000), *Conjoint Measurement: Methods and Applications* (Springer, 2000), *The Nordic School of Quality Management* (Studentlitteratur, 1999), *QFD in Theory and Practise* (in Swedish, Studentlitteratur, 1998), and *Customer Retention in the Automotive Industry: Quality, Satisfaction and Loyalty* (Gabler, 1997). In addition, Gustafsson has published over fifty academic articles, book chapters, and industry reports. Gustafsson is currently working with a number of companies on issues including customer orientation, customer involvement, and management of customer relationships.

**Michael D. Johnson** is the D. Maynard Phelps Collegiate Professor of Business Administration and professor of marketing at the University of Michigan Business School. He received his bachelor's degree from the University of Wisconsin-Madison, his MBA from the University of Chicago, and his Ph.D. from the University of Chicago. Johnson has published over one hundred academic articles and industry reports over his academic career and has authored or coauthored five other books, including the award-winning *Improving Customer Satisfaction, Loyalty, and Profit: An Integrated Measurement and Management System* (Jossey-Bass, 2000), *New Service Development and Innovation in the New Economy* (Studentlitteratur, 2000), and *Customer Orientation and Market Action* (Prentice Hall, 1998).

Johnson has been instrumental in the development of national satisfaction indices in Sweden, the United States, and Norway and currently serves on the editorial boards of the *Journal of Consumer Research,* the *Journal of Service Research,* and the *International Journal of Research in Marketing.* He teaches in both the MBA and executive education programs at Michigan and works with a variety of companies and public agencies on issues pertaining to customer and service strategy, product and service quality improvement, product and service development, and customer satisfaction measurement and relationship management. He is a member of the American Marketing Association and the Association for Consumer Research.

# Index